FIRST TWENTY

A true and inspiring story

about overcoming real adversity

TYLER BURT

Copyright 2019 by Tyler Burt

All rights reserved. This book or any portion thereof may not be reproduced or used in any manner whatsoever without the express written permission of the publisher except for the use of brief quotations in a book review.

This story is entirely based on real life events, and while all efforts have been made to ensure accuracy, some names and identifying details have been changed to protect the privacy of individuals.

Printed in the United States of America

First Printing, August 2019

ISBN 978-0-578-55605-5

Published by: Tyler Burt

TABLE OF CONTENTS

BOOK I: HOW IT ALL BEGAN **6**
    Year One.. 7
    Year Two 11

BOOK II: THE PRESCHOOL YEARS **14**
    Year Three... 15
    Year Four 25

BOOK III: THE LOWER SCHOOL YEARS........................... **28**
    Year Five 29
    Year Six 33
    Year Seven 37
    Year Eight 41
    Year Nine 47
    Year Ten 51
    Year Eleven 59

BOOK IV: THE MIDDLE SCHOOL YEARS........................... **66**
    Year Twelve.. 67
    Year Thirteen 73
    Year Fourteen 77
    Year Fifteen.. 79

BOOK V: THE HIGH SCHOOL YEARS.............................. **84**
    Year Sixteen 85
    Year Seventeen 91
    Year Eighteen... 95
    Year Nineteen 101

BOOK VI: THE COLLEGE YEAR & MORE **104**
    Year Twenty 105
    Moving Forward 113

Acknowledgments

To my Family,

Thank you. Words cannot describe how much you all have done for me. I am, and forever will be, grateful. I love you.

And for Pop,

Rest in peace. Thank you for your unrequited love, your many years of hard work, and your constant dedication to the Burt family. I love you Pop. We miss you.

Foreword

It is your reaction to adversity,
not the actual adversity itself,
that determines how
your life story will develop.

Dieter F. Uchtdorf

BOOK I

HOW IT ALL BEGAN

(11/24/1998)

Year One

My story begins in Newtown Square, PA. I was born on the morning of November 24th, 1998, in Paoli Hospital to my parents, Tom and Susan Burt. While in-utero, I miraculously survived an ischemic stroke. Although the stroke was acute, it occurred because of intermittent and decreased oxygen flow to my brain. An "acute ischemic stroke" is when a concentrated part of the brain dies due to lack of oxygen. This kind of stroke often results in paralysis of one side or severe disability for survivors. At the time, my mother's obstetrician was unable to diagnose the issue because my stroke had no outward effect on my body. I looked "healthy" during birth, and so my parents were under the impression that I was doing well. I was discharged from the hospital without a second thought and traveled home with my parents, just like any other healthy newborn. My parents were thrilled with the birth of their first son, and I immediately became a cause for celebration in our household. In the coming weeks, I was serenaded with visits from different family members and close friends. It was a joyful time for our entire family!

My family and I lived on Roberts Road in a beautiful suburb of Philadelphia. That home holds most of my earliest and some of my best childhood memories. At this age, I had little to no realization of my disability. My days consisted of playing with my parents, exploring the house, and traveling to visit my grandmother. I spent a great deal of time at my grandmother's house in South Jersey because my mother worked in the nearby family business. For the most part, I was a happy and cheerful kid. My mother fondly remembers my excitement and willingness to go to my grandmother's and play with her toys, books, and also my cousins. Life was great.

Six months later, my mother first started to become concerned. When I played with toys or tried moving around the house, I would predominantly use my left hand. It was odd. I never used my right hand for anything; it kind of just hung by my side. We met with Dr. Whoeling, and as my six-month checkup ended, my mother mentioned my left-hand dominance. The doctor was skeptical and said that it was unusual for a baby of my age to choose a dominant hand. To test her theory, the doctor held a marker about a foot away from my right shoulder. She fully expected me to grab the marker with my right hand, but unfortunately, I did not. I reached over with my left hand and grabbed the marker from her outstretched palm, almost as if my right hand did not even exist. She freaked out and immediately recommended that we see a neurologist. An MRI was needed to confirm the suspicion of a brain injury. We spent the rest of the day in the hospital, and the results of the MRI revealed that I had indeed suffered and survived an ischemic stroke. *Brain Damage. How did this happen??* My parents were shocked, sullen, and scared to death. They could not understand how an issue of this magnitude had not been discovered until now.

My mother was a wreck, but the results confirmed that the only part of my brain affected by the stroke was the left primary motor cortex. This part of the brain is responsible for controlling movement on my right side. And within the motor cortex, the doctors thought that only a single blood vessel had collapsed. Everyone was astonished. My particular brain injury is unusual and typically carries a much worse prognosis. The specialists went on to tell my parents that it was going to be impossible to predict how my injury would develop since every person is different, and every brain injury is different. They said that I would most likely have hemiparesis (paralysis) on my right side and that it could also develop into a severe disability. My parents were devastated, but tried to look on the bright side. *We have to get through this.* My mother recalls thinking. *It is going to be okay.* My parents spent the ride home praying that I would be able to overcome my injury.

Since my parents were relatively uninformed about the effects of my stroke when we left the doctor's office that day, they had to take a couple of days to process the news. They knew that I was going to be different, and yet they chose not to focus on how I was different. They loved me, anyway. They decided to acknowledge my disability and build up from there, rather than try to change me or act like it did not exist. They wanted to make sure that I was going to be okay. I was stable and seemed to be doing well, but my parents feared for what the future would hold. *Would I have another stroke? Would I be able to lead a healthy life?* It was impossible to predict what was going to happen.

On the car ride home from the hospital, my parents decided that they were going to raise me as if I was healthy. I was a lovable kid who could not keep a smile off my face. I loved playing with trains and exploring new places. If I was to survive this brain injury and did not develop a disability, my parents wanted to give me a normal childhood. They did not want to deprive me of future experiences. My parents have been my biggest supporters and have always had my best interests in mind. They promised themselves that they would raise me just like any other kid.

By the time I was almost a year old, my crawling slowly turned into walking. Unfortunately, I fell more than usual because of the weakness of my right leg. My mother filmed from a distance as I tried putting weight on my right side to get up from the ground. I cried and fell often, but never quit in the pursuit of trying to walk and run. I always bounced right back up and tried again. I never let failure deter me. My parents often took me for walks down our driveway and parts of our street. Getting to walk on harsh terrain was beneficial because it helped build muscle on my right side. While in the middle of one of these walks, my mother and I met Cindy Hoekstra. Cindy was our next-door neighbor and had recently given birth to her third child, a young boy named Carter.

Carter was born on April 4th, only a few months younger than me, and lived in the house directly across the street from us. He quickly became my best friend, and I am thankful that we are still close to this day. Through this newfound friendship with the Hoekstras, my parents and I were introduced to Aunt Carrie. 'Aunt' Carrie worked as a nanny for most of the families in the neighborhood. I met her on my first ever play-date with Carter and thankfully, she immediately accepted me as one of her own. Carrie watched from the kitchen as Carter and I played with trains for several hours and chased each other through every room in his house. It seemed like he never ran out of energy, and I always tried my best to keep up. We loved playing with each other and would move from one sport to the next, almost like clockwork. Even though we never knew what we were doing, we were always doing it together. And that is the only thing that seemed to matter. From that play-date on, Carter and I were pretty much inseparable. We began to develop a genuine friendship and watched as time flew by. He would stay over my house for hours one day, and I would do the same thing at his home

The First Twenty

the next. It was a much simpler time in my life, and also a time where I was truly happy. I was surrounded by my family's love and affection. I had made my first real friend, and I was taking the ups and downs of life day by day. I did not care about making mistakes or falling when I was knocked down. Every day was a new day.

Year Two

Before I knew it, I was already celebrating my first birthday. My parents celebrated by dancing with friends and family. The day was beautiful, and from the pictures of the smile on my face, I could not have been happier. I sat in my high-chair and ate cake while my extended family and friends brought over presents. They eagerly lined up to join in on the celebration. At the end of the party, my father shot a video of my cousins singing me happy birthday. You can see Carter sitting on the high-chair directly next to me; I do not think we left each other's side the entire day.

I spent the evening on the floor of my dining room opening presents with Carter and my cousins. We could hardly contain our excitement as we opened boxes filled with toy cars and model trains. We could not wait to play with our brand new toys. I raced my toy trains around the floor, while Carter raced his cars on our dining room table. We spent hours trying new combinations of trains and cars, loving every second of the birthday party. As my extended family began to leave, Carter and I quickly found ourselves alone on the living room floor. We chased each other around for a couple of minutes before his mother came to pick him up. I was sad to see him leave, but also extremely grateful to have had him around me at all times. He always knew how to cheer me up and how to make me laugh. I am pretty sure I developed my competitive nature from him—he was like a brother to me.

Despite my disability, my early years were similar to any other adolescent. I was in constant Physical Therapy (PT) and Occupational Therapy (OT), but most of the exercises were based on exciting activities that almost immediately became a regular part of my day. Since my parents were planning to send me to St. David's Nursery School for the upcoming year, completing the therapy gave me the confidence to start preschool. St. David's was located just five minutes from my house, and my parents were beyond excited for the start of my academic and social journey.

Vivid memories of these years were when my family and I traveled to my father's parents' house in Baltimore, Maryland, and stayed in my grandparents' spare bedroom. I grew closer to my father's brother, Uncle David, and his family. David is married to my Aunt Janet, and the pair have two kids together, Zoe and Austin. Austin, David and Janet's youngest son, is only a year and a half older than me. For the duration of the trip, my parents compared my development to Austin's and slowly started to realize just how apparent my differences were becoming. While my left hand was pointing at objects around the house and playing with toys, my right hand stayed locked in a slightly open ball.

Two weeks before my birthday, my mother gave birth to her second child, my sister Caroline. For a little while, it was tough adjusting to a new member of the family. Carrie had to be around twice as much, and we almost stopped going to South Jersey altogether. Caroline was calmer and easier to raise than I was. She hardly ever got upset and rarely cried. For me, the birth of my sister meant that I was not going to get the attention that I had been used to. She was now the topic of every conversation and my family's top priority. But honestly, I was okay with it. I have come to realize that every member of your family is a blessing. I will never forget the first time I sat with Caroline on my lap or the first time I raced one of my trains against her. She has always loved and supported me despite my disability; I could not be more grateful. The day Caroline was brought home from the hospital was the day that my parents discovered they were going to have a lot more responsibility. They were raising two kids, working full-time, and also helping me overcome my daily challenges.

Days later, my mother called a rehab doctor at CHOP. We set up an appointment and found out that despite suffering a stroke, I was actually growing normally and was quite healthy. Before leaving the office, my doctors decided to administer shots of Botox to different areas on my right side. Both my doctors and my parents believed that these Botox shots were necessary for my development. They released tightness in my muscles and would allow me to put more weight on my right side when I walked. I was able to balance on my feet more evenly and did not fall on the ground as much as a result. The shots were painful, the needles were large, and I cried after leaving the doctor's office that day. But overall, at least I was doing well and was relatively healthy.

After receiving the shots, my doctors discussed ways for me and my family to deal with my disability moving forward. Dr. Whoeling suggested additional physical therapy and occupational therapy, but it was a lecture that we had heard before. *There must be something else we can do*, my mother thought as she searched avidly on the computer for complementary therapies. We were thrilled to find an experimental therapy on the internet called constraint-induced therapy. The therapy would focus on "constraining" my good hand with a cast and forcing me to use my right hand. Dr. Edward Taub, the founder of this therapy, believed that this restriction would help in attempting to stimulate different parts of my brain—specifically the left motor cortex. At the time, the therapy was only offered at the University of Alabama - Birmingham (UAB). This therapy was new and controversial, and not even recognized or offered at the prestigious Children's Hospital of Philadelphia. There were so many unanswered questions, but my parents chose to take the leap and enter me into the program. It proved to be a financial and emotional risk for our entire family. However, if there was even a small chance that I could improve, the therapy would be well worth it.

I do not remember very much from this period of my childhood but have begun to realize just how lucky I was. I have been blessed with friends and family who were always on my side. I believe that successful parenthood—and more specifically, motherhood—is the most challenging job in the world, and I am grateful for everything my mother has done for me. My parents have shown me the true meaning of love and compassion. I hope to become as great a parent as they are when I eventually become a father.

In August, the University of Alabama Birmingham called and informed my parents of an opening at the clinic for the following summer. The nurse was unbelievably excited to work with me and said that if I accepted, I would fly out to UAB on June 6, 2001, for treatment. Without a second thought, my parents accepted and we started to book flights. My mother was thrilled and almost could not contain her excitement. I was scheduled to re-enroll in preschool that September and was now booked for constraint-induced therapy for the following summer.

BOOK II

THE PRESCHOOL YEARS

(9/15/2001)

Year Three

I started my first day of preschool at St. David's on September 6, 2001. I was scheduled to be dropped off at 8:45 AM, but I screamed when my mother got to the end of the car line and refused to get out of her car. She pulled over to the side and let the traffic pass by. "Tyler... it is your first day. It is time to go. Now." And even though her tone was stern, I did not budge. I stayed put and started to cry. I did not want to leave my mother; I just wanted to go home. When my mother reached into the back of our car and yanked my car seat forward, I finally realized I would have to go. She and Ms. Loren, the principal, nudged me through the front doors and dropped me in the classroom. I sat in school that day and barely said a word. I felt like I had been dragged out of the car against my will. I just wanted to be back home.

Towards the end of the first week, I started to open up in school and began talking to my classmates. I was able to find a group of boys that enjoyed playing with trains and cars as much as I did. We started racing our cars against each other almost every day, and I was able to form genuine friendships. We would play together for hours upon hours, and eventually, I felt as though I had become a part of their group. I became talkative and energetic. I now realize that it was easier to make friends back then because younger children are more inclusive. They did not recognize that I had a disability. From day one, they saw me as "normal," and I was never inclined to tell them anything different. My disability was not very apparent, and therefore, easier to hide, but I am happy to say that I was able to make friends that I still have to this day. I grew closer to my friends after only a couple of weeks at school. I woke up excited and ready to play with them every single day. It felt like we were always willing to do something different. One day we would race our cars against each other, and the next we would all play with Legos. Even though I still loved hanging out with my neighborhood friend Carter, I realized that I enjoyed playing with new friends as well.

After my first car line episode, my mother was nervous about dropping me off at school and asked Carrie to do it instead. She happily agreed and came to our house almost every day at 8:30 in the morning.

The First Twenty

Carrie would sit in the driveway with her car running and wait for my mother to put me in the backseat. She would drop me to Carrie on her way out of the house and always kissed me on the head before leaving. Carrie and I consistently arrive at school fifteen minutes early, and she never missed a day of pickup. Our schedule moved almost like clockwork. I grew closer to Carrie on those car rides to school, and it seemed like she always knew how to make me smile. I would never cry when I was in the car with her, and my mother was shocked because I never had another car line episode. Drop-offs with Carrie became more and more routine as each day passed. I was able to overcome my fear of school without my mother and became more independent.

Some of the teachers noticed my disability early on and began asking questions. They asked my parents why my right hand stayed curled in a ball down by my side, while my left hand seemed to do almost everything. Without hesitation, my mother was upfront and told the school about my stroke, but also asked them not to treat me any differently. She had promised to give me a normal childhood and was trying to stick to her word. The teachers agreed wholeheartedly. They watched as I continued to grow and applauded as I started developing a normal routine. From then on, they rarely talked about my disability, and my classmates were simply too young to notice. I felt like just another ordinary kid.

On my birthday, we were surprised by visits from friends and family. They brought gifts for me as well as for my parents. Uncle Doug drove up with my grandmother, who we affectionately nicknamed Mom-Mom, and the rest of his family. I was thrilled to see them. It had been months since I had raced trains against Zachary in the corner of Mom-Mom's dining room. We celebrated for about two hours before Uncle David arrived with presents and dessert. Uncle David brought his family and Gamme and Pop, my father's parents, along as well. Gamme and Pop were more than excited to spend the day doing arts and crafts with me and loved having the opportunity to hold Caroline. My parents joined in the celebration and let Carter and I run wild around the house. We played basketball against Austin, tried arts and crafts with Zoe and Sydney, and raced cars against Zachary. We were all over the place, but that is how it was supposed to be. We loved every second of it.

Although my limp was getting worse, my teachers continued to act like it did not exist. I kept on using my left hand to accomplish most tasks, and surprisingly, none of my classmates noticed. In the spring, I started learning how to read and was fascinated by the books our teachers would read to us for story time. Even though my "words" were just one syllable sounds, I was able to improve my vocabulary a little more with each passing day. I carried on playing with my friends and living a "normal" life until the end of the school year.

Summer rolled around, and my daily routine did not change much. After a few weeks, it was finally time to leave for the stroke rehabilitation clinic in Alabama. My mother packed our bags and told me about the flight to Birmingham a day before we were supposed to leave. She waited until the last possible second to tell me about the flight because my parents did not want to have to endure another one of my crying fits. They understood how much this clinic was going to help me, and they were not taking any chances. On the ride to the airport, my father told me that he could not come to UAB with me. He was going to stay home to take care of Caroline at night and needed to go to work during the day. He dropped us off at the airport and hugged me goodbye. I watched the image of my father disappear as my mother took me up the escalator and toward the security line. In all honesty, the flight was relatively uneventful. We landed, collected our suitcases, and rented a black Lexus from Enterprise Rent-A-Car. We drove twenty minutes outside of the city to the clinic and were surprised to find our names on the outside of a quaint business office on the second floor of a corporate square. When we checked in, the receptionist introduced us to the head of the program. Dr. Rostri was the clinic's leading physical therapist, and we were told that one of her associates would be working with me every day. Her assistants gave me a physical examination and made sure that my vitals were normal.

Out of the corner of my eye, I saw them preparing a cast for my arm. I pointed at her and started to shake my head. I did not know what to expect. 15 minutes later, the therapists brought the cast over and molded it on my left arm - my GOOD arm! I was dumbfounded. The cast went from the middle of my bicep down to the tips of my fingers. I squirmed and even started to cry. I did not know what to do—my left hand meant everything to me. When one of the therapists finished molding the cast, she gave me a hug. I'll never forget what she

The First Twenty

said to me, "Tyler... We are going to retrain your brain. We are going to retrain your brain so that you might be able to use your right hand more. I promise it will be okay." She told me that she would cut the cast off of my left arm in six weeks, when the clinic finished. I was speechless. Until then, I had to learn to do everything with my right hand.

I was shocked. For most of my life, my right hand had been clenched in a ball and kept at my side because I was embarrassed by my disability. But now, my life had been flipped on its head. Everything was different. There was no telling how long it would take for me to accomplish a simple task. The muscles in my right hand were weak, and I had very little dexterity. I could not change the channel on the television remote or scratch my face. Hell, I could barely even move any of my fingers. I started to cry. I could not understand why the therapist was forcing me to use my right hand. I felt utterly helpless and tried lashing out. I tried to crack the cast by punching the wall with my left hand, but it was no use. The cast did not budge, and I just ended up hurting my hand on the wall. I fell back to the floor and stared at my mother. We were stunned; it was a nightmare. My mother, with a tear in her eye, told me that the next six weeks were going to be extremely difficult, but that we would get through it together.

I wiped the tears from my eyes and realized that I was going to have to start from the very beginning. I was going to have to learn to do everything, and I mean everything, again. It was apparent that I was frustrated and so my therapists decided to begin my therapy with tip-to-tip. Tip-to-tip is supposed to be a relatively simple exercise where you touch your pointer finger to your thumb repeatedly; however, it was not simple for me. I spent the entire first day just on the exercise and had very little success. I was not able to bend my thumb so that it touched my pointer finger. It was frustrating. And even though I felt defeated, I knew that I would never give up. I did not want to disappoint my mother.

At the end of the first night, a therapist asked me to pick up the television remote and press ten on its keypad. I spent ten minutes just trying to pick up the remote, and even then, I had to call my mother to change the channel. I did not have the dexterity that was necessary to push the buttons down. I started to cry and fell to the floor. I buried my face in my hands. I did not know what was wrong with me. Multiple therapists picked me up from the floor and gave me a hug. "It is okay to get frustrated," they told me. "But we're going to get through this. We are going to get through this together. You are going to get better. Give it time. All we have to do is keep trying. I promise it will get better." They walked me to bed. My mother followed them in and gave me a kiss goodnight. I stopped crying. At that moment, I realized that I could be in the fight of my life.

Every morning for the next four weeks, I practiced tip-to-tip for two hours with my mother and multiple therapists before breakfast. One of the therapists told me that the goal of the exercise was to stimulate the fingertips to see if we could 'wake up the nerves'. The process was frustrating, and I continued to have very little success. I began looking to my mother for comfort, and thankfully, she was always there to hold my hand. It was because of her support that I was able to persevere. I started noticing slight improvements in my abilities with each passing day, and the therapists realized that my brain was starting to find ways to circumnavigate the damaged parts of itself. My therapist's words from the first day were slowly starting to come true. I was finally beginning to retrain my brain through rehabilitation.

After finishing the tip-to-tip exercise, I would immediately try to pour myself a bowl of Cinnamon Toast Crunch for breakfast. I tried hundreds of times, but unfortunately, I was never successful. I did not have enough strength or dexterity to pour the milk into the bowl and was barely able to raise the spoon to my mouth. The therapist and my mom had to feed me breakfast every morning. I was embarrassed, and yet there was little that I could do to change the situation. My left hand was incapacitated; I felt helpless. When I finished breakfast, the therapist brought me into the living room and laid out different tasks for me to do for that particular day. And although the tasks often varied, they seemed to accomplish the same goal. One day the therapist would ask me to turn ten pages in a book, and the next I would have to twist and turn a wooden doorknob. The daily exercises proved to be extremely difficult. I would often fail for hours and hours before making even a tiny breakthrough. But, I never let myself get too discouraged and ultimately learned how to persevere. At the end of each session, my therapists would throw me a hack-e-sac to cheer me up. They told my mother and me that it would improve my dexterity and hand-eye coordination. I tried tossing it up like a baseball while lying on the table, and soon it became my favorite toy.

For lunch, I would consistently have either grilled cheese or a peanut butter and jelly sandwich. Any meal that required a fork and a knife proved to be too challenging to eat. And even then, I almost always ended up crushing the sandwich with my fingers. I would squeeze the jelly everywhere and made a mess in the kitchen. Eventually, I ended up having to ask my mother to help feed me the sandwich. She agreed, and then we would go right back to work. I spent the rest of my day completing menial tasks around our apartment and trying to improve my dexterity. I did everything from pointing at the door to picking up Q-tips and playing board games. Once I had seen the progress I could make in such a short amount of time, I was convinced that the therapy was working. My mood brightened as I slowly started to build muscle memory on my right side. My right hand was no longer curled up in a ball and shoved to my side; it was slowly making progress in doing everyday things.

When the therapists and my mother cooked dinner for me every night, it was much of the same story. I was not very strong enough to hold a fork in my right hand and had a hard time getting food in my mouth. And though we rarely talked at the table because I was exhausted from the day's therapy, my mother would try to fill the silence by getting me to practice tip-to-tip. She was relentless. It did not matter how much I complained or how much I cried; she never gave me a day off. Only now have I begun to realize that my mother was always willing to put my happiness above her own. It never bothered her how much I screamed at her; she just wanted me to get better. After finishing dinner, I would move to the couch and watch Bob the Builder on the television. My therapists would always stay at the table and discussed the plan for the upcoming day with my mother. I was allowed to watch about a half an hour of television before my mother read me a bedtime story and put me to bed. I consistently fell asleep as soon as my head hit the pillow. Even though I have always been scared to sleep in new places, I got through each night without any trouble. I woke up every morning re-energized and ready to start a new day.

One night towards the end of our third week, the therapist introduced my mother and me to a desktop computer. She explained each of the keys to me and opened up a blank word document. My mother picked me up and put me on the therapist's lap. They sat me in front of the computer and asked me to type. I did not know it yet, but typing was going to be the most frustrating and challenging exercise that I had ever done. We started the task by having my mother say the letter to me out loud and subsequently point it out on the keyboard. Even with all of my improvement, I quickly discovered that my pointer finger was the only finger that could apply enough pressure to press any key on the keyboard down. The goal of the exercise was to work on my finger's dexterity, and my therapists wanted me to type my name out on the word document, over and over again. I failed many times before I was even able to type out the first two letters of my name. Not only did I struggle to locate where the letters were on the keyboard, but I would also sometimes press two keys by mistake. I tried out the computer for a week and became increasingly upset; I felt like I was not making any progress. The therapists would always delete my work after two hours and make me start again. I felt like a failure. I could not even type out my first name. The computer quickly became my arch nemesis. I tried to do everything in my power to avoid it, but every day, the therapists kept bringing me back to the same chair. If I told them I was going to give up, they would start to hide the television remote until I stopped complaining. I felt like I was in hell. Some days I would spend two hours on the computer, and on other days I would spend four. There was no telling how long it would take me to type out my name, and that is why I was always upset. I started to feel like I could not make any progress. It was demoralizing.

While watching Sesame Street one night, I was surprised by a visit from my father and Caroline. I was thrilled to see them. I started crying immediately; they were a sight for sore eyes. I could not wait to introduce my father to my therapy team and show him around the clinic. The next day, he joined my mother and me as we went through my daily routine. He observed as I pointed out the doors in the room and repeatedly tried to turn a wooden doorknob. He was shocked to see how much I had improved in only a month. I have always sought my father's approval, and his arrival gave me new motivation. I began to ramp up my therapy. I was no longer scared to drop a fork in the kitchen did not care if the food never reached my mouth. I attacked the computer with a newfound intensity every day. I wanted my father to see me improve, and I was not scared to fail in front of him. My competitive nature must have kicked in. By the time my father and sister had reached the clinic, my cast no longer bothered me. It had simply become a part of my daily routine. I went through my exercises without giving it a second thought.

By the time I had finished the fourth week, I had started making some substantial breakthroughs. I finally learned how to hold a fork and simultaneously raise the food into my mouth. My family was overjoyed. They cheered me on and could not wait to congratulate me. I was slowly "rewiring" my brain, and my therapists were thrilled. My family and I rode this newfound confidence into the final weeks of my stay at UAB. Weeks five and six were referred to as the "closing weeks" of my therapy. The therapists told my family that I would no longer be learning any new exercises. Instead, they said that we were going to spend the last two weeks reviewing the progress that I had already made. I was excited; I would finally be able to show everyone the extent of my improvement. Looking back, I am incredibly grateful to UAB and all of their therapists. They helped me accomplish more than anyone ever thought could be possible.

On the second to the last day of my stay at the clinic, the therapist cut the cast off of my left hand. I was scared by the size and shape of the saw but eventually found myself screaming in excitement. I turned my palm up and down so many times that I got dizzy. I remember flexing my fingers for hours to make sure that they were mine. I spent most of that day on the computer and learned how to type with both hands. With my left hand available, I efficiently ran through my daily routine and was able to correctly type my name into a word document in less than an hour. I was overcome with emotion; I was finally back! I began to feel like myself again.

Later in the evening, my family and I packed our bags and prepared for our flight back home to Philadelphia. We woke up at 6:00 AM and said our goodbyes to every therapist in the office. I thanked each of my therapists and hugged them before my mother quickly ushered me to the car. I did not know it yet, but the "never give up" mentality that I had learned over those six weeks proved to play a significant role in all of the achievements in my life. I learned how to persevere and how to get back up after being knocked down. I realize now that the clinic was an essential building block in my life. I am grateful to the entire UAB team for all of their hard work. I am not sure I would be where I am today without them.

When my family and I arrived home from Alabama, we officially started our summer. I was overly excited to be home. I could not wait to see Carter. When we returned, I unconsciously started using my left hand more than my right. I did attempt to use my right hand for various tasks around the house, but eventually realized that I was able to accomplish everything more efficiently and more quickly if I just used my left hand. It felt more natural. I fell into a routine and stood by as my left hand started to become dominant once again. As the summer flew by, my mother reminded me to use my right hand around the house and forced me to practice tip-to-tip with her every day. For the rest of our summer, we spent most of our time either at home or visiting our cousins. I played with friends, enjoyed the summer weather, and continued my therapy. I probably should have kept using my right hand for menial tasks around the house, but unfortunately, I did not. It was still difficult to do almost everything with my right hand, and I was afraid to show my friends that I was different. I thought that they were going to judge me, I was afraid to lose them. From then on, I decided that I would try to appear as "normal" as possible. If that meant letting my left hand become my dominant hand, then so be it.

Year Four

I started my second year at Saint David's on September 7th, 2002. I was excited to go back to school so that I could see my old friends and learn about my new teachers. It was no longer a struggle for me to get dropped off every morning, and I always left the car with a smile. That year, I made a couple of new friends and started looking to broaden my horizons. Of course, I loved racing trains and cars, but I began to develop a strong love for reading. "Personal reading time" was easily my favorite class of the day. It was a time where I could zone everyone else out and simply relax. I tried to read every book that I could get my hands on. Most nights, my mother and I would pick out a story to read before bedtime. It was always something that I could look forward to. My father would sometimes sit in on the readings with my mother, but he was usually downstairs working or taking care of my sister Caroline.

The year slowly dragged on. I continued with my daily routine and completed my therapy exercises almost every day while my parents decided where to send me for Elementary school. I walked over to Carter's house regularly and would play basketball or race trains with him in his basement. When my parents needed a night out, Carrie would bring Carter over to my house. We would watch television in my living room and run through the backyard for hours.

On Thanksgiving, my family and I made the hike to South Jersey to visit my mother's side of the family. I had not been to Mom-Mom's house in months because of St. David's. I could not wait to play with Zachary and Sydney. I have always loved visiting my extended family. For Christmas break, my family and I made another trip to visit our cousins. This time, we drove to Towson to visit my father's side of the family. I was thrilled to spend time with Gamme and Pop. I loved painting shells and playing croquet with them in their backyard. On this trip, my cousin Austin and I became close. I would chase him around the yard for hours, and we would always race our cars against each other until my parents called us inside for dinner. We stayed in Maryland for a few days before making the trip up to Uncle David's "mountain" house in Freedom, New Hampshire.

The house, only a five-minute drive from Ossipee Lake, was often the highlight of our summer. My family would always stay at the mountain house for at least a week every year, and I loved being able to spend quality time with my grandparents and cousins. While at the "mountain house," Austin and I continued hanging out and having fun. And though he never once commented on my disability, he did always ask about my night splint. The splint, which Dr. Whoeling had given to me a week before we drove up to New Hampshire, was bulky and ugly. And although it did its job, it could not completely correct the extent of my supination. To the untrained eye, I looked almost normal - except for the fact that I walked with a slight hitch in my step. I was extremely embarrassed about it and tried to hide my disability from my extended family. I was ashamed to tell my parents about how I felt, not knowing that they had, of course, already told the entire family about my stroke. But I did not know that. I never spoke up, and therefore had to suffer in silence. *Would this change the way they treated me? Would they no longer want to talk to me? Would they no longer wish to see me?* A million questions came to mind. At the time, I did not realize that the anxiety was all in my head. My family already knew about my stroke. They loved me anyway. They loved me for me, for who I was, but my subconscious told me otherwise.

In the spring, I was introduced to the sport of Lacrosse. My father was playing for an M.A.B. Paints team when my mother and I decided to drive up and see the game. My father and his side of the family grew up on Lacrosse. My grandfather, Pop, played midfield at the University of Maryland and was a member of the 1959 National Championship team. My Uncle David played at Dartmouth. My father played at the University of Virginia and later professionally for the Philadelphia Wings. I watched him from the sidelines and immediately fell in love with the sport of Lacrosse.

I finished the school year at St. David's and tried to improve my listening skills. I was an early reader, and my vocabulary was expanding, but I never seemed to listen to what others had to say. I would always interrupt or try to interject with my thoughts. As I reflect on this, it might have had something to do with me trying to mask and deal with my disability.

As the summer rolled around, I strengthened the relationships with my friends from St. David's and tried to have them over for playdates as much as possible. During the school year, I had become best friends with two boys from my class, Ryan and Colin. I considered myself lucky. I'll admit, I had problems telling the truth and listening to others, but have always been able to make friends. Ryan, Colin, and I hung out together almost every day, and the two did not know, or maybe did not care, about my disability. I spent my free time either doing tip-to-tip and working on my right hand's dexterity or playing games in the living room with my sister.

Towards the end of July, my mother introduced me to two different families, the Schreder's and the Gunsalus'. They were best friends of my parents, and each had a son about my age. I met the Schreders first. Parents Steve and Maria gave birth to their oldest son Andrew just three months before I was born. Not long after, I was introduced to Curt and Courtney Gunsalus. They had also given birth to their oldest son, Connor, in September of 1998—he was only two months older than me. Our parents set up playdates for the three of us often, and soon we all became close friends. At the time, I did not feel like I was any less of a person than them. We liked the same activities and looked at the world the same way. I was thankful that they did not see me much differently than they saw themselves.

In early August, my mother surprised me after dinner and told me that I was no longer going to attend St. David's. She hugged me and said that I would start at The Episcopal Academy in pre-kindergarten for the upcoming school year. I remember sprinting to my room as the tears began to swell up in my eyes. I was unsure of what the future would bring. I was no longer going to see my friends from St. David's every day, I would have to start fresh. *What would my new friends think about me? Would they notice my disability?* The questions gave me an uneasy feeling in the pit of my stomach. I winced at the idea of going alone. I was too scared that my new classmates would judge me. Two days later, I received unbelievable news. Ryan and Connor were going to be joining me at EA. I was overjoyed. The doubts that I had about going to a new school went away in an instant. I was going with two of my best friends, and I knew they would always have my back. I was sure that these pre-existing relationships were going to make my transition to Episcopal much easier. I knew that I was going to be okay.

BOOK III

THE LOWER SCHOOL YEARS

(6/7/2003)

Year Five

The first day I walked through the doors of the Episcopal Academy was September 18, 2003. The buildings were massive, and there was a certain "buzz" around the campus. I was astonished; I loved it. I met up with Connor and Ryan outside the classroom and prepared to start my first day of pre-kindergarten. I was introduced to all of my new classmates and continued trying to develop my reading skills. My circle of friends expanded, and I began to enjoy life. I had always been an energetic kid who kept a smile glued to his face, and I brought that same energy to my new school.

Unfortunately, that happiness started to slip away a bit after my first week of school. My limp had become a bit more pronounced, and I was afraid that my classmates would notice. My mother made an appointment with my rehab doctor. She gave me a higher quality night splint and an ankle brace to wear at school during the day. The brace would go under my khaki pants and keep my Achilles tendon from tightening up. I liked the look of the brace—it had a royal blue frame with a polished silver finish. I was excited when the doctor first showed it to me and could not wait to put it on. In that same appointment, I was also scheduled for another round of Botox injections in my Achilles tendon. While the Botox helped with the muscle tightness, the side-effect was a weaker muscle tone on my right side. It was now imperative that I wear my brace every night, as I began falling and tripping more than usual.

Unfortunately, I found out pretty quickly that my initial excitement was misleading. Since my brace made a squishing sound every time I walked, it ended up drawing unwanted attention from my classmates. It was upsetting. I was embarrassed about my disability and wanted to keep it a secret. Whenever a classmate asked, I always said that I had just hurt my ankle on the monkey bars. I was a coward; at the time, I could not even bring myself to tell my best friends the truth. I was too self-conscious. I did not want my classmates to judge me. I begged my parents to allow me to go to school without the brace, but weeks passed before I was able to make any headway. My parents called our doctor, and reluctantly agreed to let me stop wearing the brace to school on the condition that I begin physical therapy every week. Immediately, I said yes. I was prepared to do anything to hide the fact that I had a stroke from my new friends, and physical therapy proved to be a good compromise. I stopped wearing the brace the next day and, to my surprise, life slowly returned to normal. The questions about my right ankle dissipated and my mood quickly improved.

For the rest of the year, I developed a new daily routine and tried to stick to it. I kept playing with my friends, kept improving my reading skills, and tried to hide my "secret" from everyone. Every day at 11 AM, my teacher, Ms. Reinhart, would hold class cleanup hours after she finished her daily puppet show. We would not be dismissed to lunch until we had adequately cleaned up the entire room. I tried my best to go along with the class, but in that hour I truly found out how lazy I was. I hated cleaning up so much that I even tried to complain to my parents. My father just laughed. "That is life, Tyler. You will get used to it. Just put your head down and do the work." Of course, he was right.

I went back to school and was able to grow closer to two new classmates, Thomas Woodville and Luke O'Grady. We would swing on the monkey bars and play soccer together at recess. Connor, Ryan, Luke, and I eventually found ourselves hanging out with each other every day. We formed a friend group and started arranging playdates on the weekends. Sometimes we would play games, but our favorite activity to play together was sports. We always played different sports with one another, and I believe that is the reason why we were able to become so close as friends.

Around this time, I grew closer to Caroline and Gamme and Pop. I have always loved Caroline, and I remember feeling like it was my duty to protect my little sister. I always had to make sure she was okay; I would do anything for her. We often played tag together, and sometimes I would read her a bedtime story. When my grandparents came to the house, we would all paint seashells at the dinner table and make each other laugh. She was a much better painter than me despite her young age. And even though I was a bit jealous, I was still happy for her.

My mother gave birth to her second son, my younger brother William, on April 26, 2004. William, affectionately known to our family and friends as just "Wills," is my parent's third and youngest child. For some reason, his birth was more difficult to deal with than Caroline's. I was the oldest child in the family and not yet prepared to receive the least amount of attention. I was not ready to receive the least amount of Christmas presents or to be the last one checked on every night, but unfortunately, it happened. Uncle Doug and Aunt Kelly were the first to arrive at our house for the celebration of Wills' birth. While playing outside, I remember my cousin yelling down from the swing set almost immediately after I tried climbing on the monkey bars. "Hey, Ty... what's up? Why are you walking like that? Your ankle okay?" I turned around and ran back inside. I was embarrassed—he had no idea about my disability. *Was it that noticeable?* I struggled to grasp the true gravity of my stroke. I thought that everyone's off-hand was weaker than their dominant hand. I thought that I walked almost like a normal person. I remember banging the toes on my right foot against the corner of my bed and screaming at them to "wake up!" I started crying. I just wanted to be normal, to be like everyone else around me. At the time, I was not mature enough to understand my shortcomings. I went back to school more upset than I had ever been.

If there was a God, I could not figure out why he chose to make me this way. For a few weeks, I let the fear of rejection overcome my originality. Luckily, my friend group at school was able to lift my spirits. We constantly joked around, and they always found a way to make me laugh. With their help, I was able to build a barrier in my head. I pushed my disability to the darkest corners of my thoughts. I left it there and told myself that I would never go back. I was not ready to come face to face with my biggest obstacle. Looking back, it was not the correct response. I bottled my thoughts up and genuinely believed that I would not have to deal with them later down the line. I was wrong, but at least I was able to cheer myself up for the time being.

One day as the school year was in the process of winding down, my parents took my siblings and me to Summit, New Jersey. While there, we visited longtime friends of my parents, Kelly and John Bunting. The parents, and now their children, have become almost like family to me. Aunt Kelly and Uncle John have two sons together, Jack and James. Jack is their oldest and was born only three years after me. He is a fantastic kid and has always been close to my sister Caroline. We spent the weekend at the Bunting's house and I started to become familiar with my cousins. Jack, Caroline, and I chased each other around their swing set for hours while our parents reminisced about old stories over a glass of wine.

As I stopped chasing Caroline down the slide, I could not help but notice Jack as he completed the monkey bars. He was able to use his left hand, his off-hand, to scale the entire swing set. He hoisted himself above the monkey bars and took a seat atop the roof. I was astonished. It seemed like his hands were working together, sharing the burden of his body weight. I looked down at my hands. *My hands cannot do that. Why can't my hands do that?* I started to tear up and ran inside. I begged my mother to go home. She was skeptical, so I lied and told her that I had the stomach bug. My parents questioned my excuse, but eventually gave in to my demands when they realized that I was not going to stop complaining. On the car ride home, they asked me about my stomach bug over and over again. I told them that I must have eaten some rotten food and chose to hide my real feelings. I was not yet ready to share my insecurities with anyone. I did not want my parents to think that I was weak or soft in any way. I have come to realize that I made the wrong decision. I should have asked for their help; I should have let them in sooner.

Year Six

I started my first day of kindergarten at Episcopal on September 18, 2004. I was able to keep the same friend group throughout the summer, but unfortunately, we were placed in different classes to start the school year. Ryan and I had Ms. Page for a teacher, while Luke and Connor were in Mrs. Welsh's class down the hall. At the year's introductory assembly, I desperately needed to go to the bathroom and called across the gym for my teacher, "Ms. Page… Ms. Page… Ms. Page!" I tried to make a scene but was met with silence. It was clear that she could not hear me. I made the wrong decision and decided to yell her first name into the crowd, and I yelled it loud. "Twiggy!" I stomped my foot on the floor and tried to get her attention. The crowd immediately fell silent, and everyone started to turn towards me Ms. Page rushed over and yanked me into the hallway. She was noticeably upset, but she had a reason to be. I had been disrespectful.

I apologized profusely, but my words were met with a stone-cold gaze. Ms. Page sat me outside of the principal's office. "You are in timeout. Sit here. Don't you dare move." I felt awful. I immediately obliged and took the seat furthest away from the entrance to our principal's office. I sat there in silence for what seemed like hours but was probably only minutes. Suddenly, I felt a tap on my left shoulder. "Hey, whaddya in here for?" I realized that the voice belonged to a new classmate of mine. I had been introduced to him earlier that morning. He moved over and took a seat right next to me, extending his hand out to give me a high-five. "I am Alex McLaughlin. We met this morning. What's your name again?" I laughed and introduced myself. "Well, Tyler… Whaddya here for?" As I began to tell the story, our principal swung her door open. "Alex McLaughlin? Alex McLaughlin? Please come in." I hit him on the shoulder and pointed towards her office. "Bye man. I'll see you later. Good luck. I hope everything's okay."

Fifteen minutes later, Ms. Page came back into the office and told me to stand up. "You're out of timeout. Let's go. We are going back to class." I was scared as I rose from the chair, thinking that she was going to yank my shoulder and forcefully pull me back to the classroom. I blurted out another apology. "I'm so sorry. I'm so sorry. I made a mistake." She cut me off and lowered her tone. "Promise me that you will never do that again." I nodded. She grabbed my hand and walked me back to class. "We all make mistakes. It's okay." She forgave me and showed me to the bathrooms. As I got back to the classroom, I saw Ryan talking to Alex. I jogged up to them and told them why I had just gotten in trouble. I thought that they would be sympathetic, but they just started laughing. I did not know that Ryan and Alex were already close friends. Ms. Page put Alex in my cleanup group that day, and we quickly built a friendship. He started racing cars with me in the morning and played soccer with my friends and me during recess. He was an energetic kid who loves to make others laugh. I enjoyed having him around because he always made me forget about my disability. If I was not playing with friends, I was in the classroom trying to improve my reading and writing skills. I used the majority of my free time to read most of the books we had lying around the classroom and started learning how to write. I improved my vocabulary and spent the rest of the school year to develop a new daily routine.

In the spring, my parents bought my siblings and me our first basketball hoop. I was thrilled; the hoop was a plastic *Little Tikes EasyScore Basketball Set* for kids. I can still picture it today. My parents decided to get it for us after watching Carter and I constantly dribble a basketball on the living room floor. Whether it was playing one on one, trying to dunk on each other or just shooting around, we slowly became attached to that hoop. I have had a competitive personality from an early age, and basketball was a way for me to show it. As the school year turned to summer, Carter and I started dragging the hoop out of the house and to the backyard so that we could enjoy the warm weather. Basketball became a way for Carter and me to bond. We loved competing. At least one of us would be practicing on the hoop every single day, no matter the circumstances. I quickly realized that I was starting to fall in love with the game of basketball.

My family and I spent almost the entire month of July visiting our cousins and grandparents. We stayed at Mom-Mom's house in Rosenhayn for a week before driving up to Uncle David's house in Freedom. We enjoyed Ossipee Lake with our extended family, and I spent most of the week learning how to waterski. Even though it was enjoyable, actually getting up on the skis proved to be much more difficult than it looked. Austin always popped up right away, but I was never able to. I used to hate how my father and Uncle David cheered him on from the boat. I could not help it; I wanted that to be me. I wanted him to be the one in the boat cheering me on.

For the next week, we went out on the boat every day, and I tried a couple more times to get up on the skis. I practiced my pop up on the sand and figured out ways to re-distribute the majority of my weight to my left side. I figured out how to balance myself on top of the water so that I could get up with only my left leg, and it actually ended up working. I popped up and planted my left leg firmly into the water behind the wake of the boat. Then, I slowly eased my weight onto my right leg and pulled on the rope as hard as I possibly could. Before I knew it, I was water skiing. It was a huge accomplishment, and I was thrilled! I had found a way to compensate for my disability. From a distance, I looked just like any other kid on the lake. My parents were overjoyed. I did not know or understand it at the time, but water skiing had unconsciously taught me that my disability was merely an obstacle. I had proven to myself that my disability could be overcome. With practice and the right attitude, I knew that could do anything. I might not be as good at certain things as everyone else, but it did not matter. I had persevered over another obstacle.

When we returned from New Hampshire, my mother decided to sign Carter and me up for a youth soccer team. We were placed on the same team, the Newtown Square Tigers, and played our games at a local indoor field. Within about two weeks, I discovered that I did not enjoy soccer as much as I thought I would. The game felt slow, and I often grew bored when playing defense. The action always seemed so far away, and I could not be as physical as I wanted to be. Even though I did not like the particular sport, I learned that I loved being part of a team. The camaraderie and togetherness of our group was unbelievable. All of my teammates had become my close friends. I finished out the summer with the Tigers and used my free time to improve my listening skills. Every night before bed, my mother, father, and I read sports books or *Brown Bear, Brown Bear What Do You See?* The stories quickly became some of my favorite books, but not because of their storylines. They became my favorites because of the one-on-one time I was able to spend with my parents. I cherished it.

Year Seven

I started my first day of first grade on September 6, 2005. Connor and I were placed in Mrs. Spofford's class, while the rest of our friend group was across the hall in Ms. Petrie's class. I was able to keep my daily routine consistent, and just added school back into the mix. I continued reading and used the rest of my free time to practice sports with my friends.

In October, Mrs. Spofford introduced our class to a new subject: mathematics. She started the first day by teaching us how to add. To me, the concept seemed unbelievably foreign and difficult to understand. It was too much to memorize; I struggled to keep up. I have always loved reading, and yet math never came easily to me. My parents and I practiced addition at the dinner table for hours and hours, but specific numbers began to frustrate me. I did not understand why we would ever have to add numbers together. It all seemed incredibly stupid.

Throughout the year, I became incredibly close with Connor because we were both in Mrs. Spofford's class. We spent a majority of our time at his house either playing basketball or climbing up his swing set. On weekends, we would barricade the longest hallway in his house, put helmets on, and run straight at each other. A mini Oklahoma drill, if you will. Alex came over to Connor's house one day after winter break and surprised us with some *Pokémon* cards. Connor and I had no idea about the world of *Pokémon*, but we decided to give it a try. We chose to start our endeavor by trading Alex a bracelet and a mini basketball for Squirtle and Charizard. Connor brought our new merchandise into school the next day, and not surprisingly, Squirtle quickly became a hot commodity. Each one of our friends wanted to add the card to their collection.

One day after school, I traded Connor a bunch of worthless football cards for his Squirtle card. Immediately, I knew that I had won the trade and so I tried to run out of his front door with my new card. Connor quickly realized what I was in the process of doing and caught me just as I started running up the stairs. He tackled me; he wanted to implement a "trade-back" clause, but I refused to give it to him. I sidestepped his next take down and went sprinting up the stairs. He got up and threw his shoe at the back of my head. He yelled, "Tyler! Get back here now!" as I ran straight out of the front door. I was scared he was going to kill me. He picked his Merrell up off of the ground and ran after me. He chased me around the house, his right Merrell shoe in his left hand high above his head, like a madman. I screamed and ran to the backyard, where I found Connor's mother gardening. "Help me! Mrs. G... Connor might kill me!"

I dove behind her just as Connor tried to take a swipe at me. She blocked him and started screaming at both of us. She told us to knock it off and to go back inside, but Connor was relentless. I knew that was not going to stop and pleaded with Mrs. G for help. As we started explaining the story to her, she grabbed us by the shirts, dragged us inside, and put us in timeout. She separated us for an hour and eventually decided to drive me home. Connor cursed up a storm from the yard as his mother and I pulled out of his driveway. I became noticeably upset and started to bang on the window in retaliation. It was the first fight that Connor and I ever had.

That night, my mother and Mrs. G sat me down and told me how the trade that I had made to Connor was unfair. They were right, and I started to feel bad. I saw Connor in school the next day but did not actually end up talking to him until he came over for dinner that night. His mom brought him over to apologize, and I ended up giving him his Squirtle card back. I told him that I was sorry and that I should not have tried to trick him. I promised him that I would never trick him again, and thankfully, he forgave me. After dinner, we hugged each other and quickly became best friends once again.

As the year continued, writing proved to be more and more challenging because I was not able to stabilize the page with my right hand; I did not have enough dexterity in my fingers. I was upset. In one of our after school meetings, Mrs. Spofford taught me how to compensate by writing with the page at a forty-five-degree angle. That way, I could use my left wrist to stabilize the paper instead of my right hand. Her method proved to be extremely useful. I was thankful, even though it looked peculiar to almost everyone who saw me try to write. Everyone asked why I wrote sideways, but I just brushed their comments right off my shoulders. At least now I had the opportunity to excel in something other than reading. I worked incredibly hard to make my handwriting as neat as possible.

    Summer came around, and my mother decided that the only way she would allow me to try out for the school basketball team was if I started meeting with a tutor. The tutor, Ms. Jacobson, came to the house two times a week to review math concepts with me. And though the hour and a half that I spent with her felt like hell, she was fantastic at her job and we were able to make substantial progress. In those tutoring sessions, I improved my addition skills and also started learning how to subtract. We had actually learned subtraction on the second to last week of school that year, but I did not pay attention because I was too busy still trying to understand addition.

Year Eight

    I walked into my second grade class for the first time on September 18, 2006. Along with Alex and Ryan, I had been placed in Ms. Davis's class for the year. Unfortunately, Connor and Luke were in a different classroom and were placed in Mrs. Welsh's class instead of ours. I met new classmates and became familiar with all of the second-grade teachers. My mood stayed consistent, and I was happy. We reviewed subtraction and went over the summer reading on our first day of class. Luckily, I had already been prepared for Ms. Davis's lessons by Ms. Jacobson. I could not wait to show my teachers just how much I had improved. I was no longer a straggler in subjects like math and handwriting; I was one of the leaders of the pack. As I slowly settled into my environment, I realized that I had a great group of friends. I finally understood addition and subtraction, I woke up every day excited to go to school. I was happy. I told myself every morning that I could be just as good, or better, than my classmates despite my disability. If I was willing to put in the work, then I too could be successful.

    I spent the next three weeks trying to bury my head in the books, but unfortunately, I did not learn anything. I often caught myself daydreaming, and most of the schoolwork went right over my head. I stopped reading as avidly and devoted most of my free time to sports. I loved basketball and dragged my father outside to rebound for me almost every night. If he was not available, I would always walk over to Carter's house and play with him. After one of our nightly games, I walked across the street with Carter and joined his family for dinner. We were planning to spend the night playing mini hockey in his basement when his brother Chris came downstairs and surprised us with a *Game Boy Color*. Our plans flew right out the window. I still remember the first game we ever played, *Tony Hawk Pro Skater 2*. I was mesmerized by Carter's new *Game Boy* and immediately ran back home to beg my parents for one. I wanted it more than anything. I spent the next week finding every excuse to go over to Carter's house so that I could play his *Game Boy*. We lost ourselves in hours of gameplay and thought *Tony Hawk Pro Skater 2* was the greatest thing in the world!

The First Twenty

One particular Friday after school, Connor and Alex introduced me to tee-ball. They set up bases in Connor's backyard and invited me over to play. I loved learning how to bat, but not surprisingly, fielding proved to be a whole different story. I was usually pretty athletic and decent at most sports that I picked up, but that was not the case with baseball. I put the glove on my right hand and tried to field a couple of balls. Almost immediately, I knew it was not going to work. My right hand was not strong enough to fully close my glove, so I was never able to catch a baseball correctly. The ball would either hit my glove and fall out, or I would have to snag it with my left hand before it dropped to the ground. As my friends ran to pick up all of the balls from around the yard, they tried to offer me words of encouragement. I was embarrassed. No matter how hard I practiced, no matter how much effort I gave, I realized that I would never be able to catch a baseball. My right hand was not strong enough to close the glove. There was simply nothing that I could do.

Three months later, I was surprised by a visit from Carter. He walked over to my house after dinner one day and brought over a brand new 76ers themed basketball. He suggested that we play one on one. I was in a bad mood and repeatedly told him to "get lost." As soon as I initially refused, he knew something was up. I was too competitive not to accept a game of basketball, and he knew that better than anyone. He took a seat on my patio and started asking a million questions; he told me he was not going to leave until I explained why I would not play with him. I tried to argue, but he would not listen. He got up and tossed me the ball. "We are going to the hoop right now... It'll make you feel better. Trust me. " He moved the rim down, and we started to get shots up. I had not played basketball for a few weeks and quickly discovered just how rusty I was. I was not hitting anything; it was brick after brick. Carter took one of the balls to the top of the key and slammed it to the pavement.

"Let's play one on one. We need to work on our off-hands. If we don't get better now, we might never be as good as we could be. Here." He passed me the ball. "Drive on me righty. I'll play D." I winced as I began to take my first jab step. I tried to object, but he was not having any of it. I was nervous. I had never put the basketball in my right hand before; I had no idea how to dribble. He waved me towards him. "Let's go, bro. I don't have all day."

I took a deep breath. I put the ball in my right hand and attempted to dribble. I was only able to take one step toward the hoop before Carter stopped me dead in my tracks. "What are you doing, man?" He started to mock me. "Stop slapping the ball. C'mon. Be Serious." We started again. I swore I tried listening to him, but I just could not stop slapping the ball. I was upset; my disability was preventing me from being able to dribble the ball normally. I took another two steps toward the hoop before he grabbed me by the arm. "Are you even listening to me, Ty - what gives man? Listen here..." He grabbed the ball from me and started dribbling with his off-hand. "This is how you dribble with your off-hand. Stop playing with me. Try this time. I'm trying to get us better. Please."

He passed the ball back to me at the top of the key, and I prepared to drive to the hoop once again. As I put the ball in my right hand, I hit it with my palm by accident instead of trying to use my fingers like he had just shown me. "Stop. Stop." He screamed. "I am done. You do not want me to help you, fine. Don't use my help. It looks like you got everything figured out anyway." He tried to storm off of the court, but I grabbed his wrist and spun him backwards. Tears started to stream down my face.

"Look, Carter. There's something that I have to tell you," I choked the words out. "I am different than you. My right hand does not work as well as my left, and I was born that way. I can't help it. That's why I can't dribble the way you want me to." I wiggled the fingers on my left hand and then tried to wiggle the fingers on my right hand to show him that I was not lying. "I just can't do this, man, I tried as hard as I possibly could." I felt like I had been crying for hours. Snot started to drip from my nose. I wiped my eyes with my shirt, and Carter fell silent. "Well, aren't you gonna say anything?"

It was a while before he nodded. I could tell he did not know what to say. "Dang... man, that sucks. I am so sorry. I didn't mean to make fun of you earlier." His voice trailed off. He shifted his gaze to the hoop. "Maybe sports is not your thing... but that's okay. Let's go inside and play *Pokémon* instead. I'm hungry." While I was happy that he still wanted to play with me, I was struck by the realization that he did not fully understand the gravity of my situation. He ran into the garage and disappeared behind the garage door. And though I was upset, I felt like a huge weight had been lifted off of my shoulders. Carter knew that I was different, and it seemed like he did not care. He wanted to hang out with me anyway. I was thankful. It was the first time I ever told one of my friends about my stroke, and if given a choice to tell anyone, I am happy it was him.

I went back to school and finished the year in Ms. Davis's class. I read a new book almost every week, but unfortunately, I also began to fall behind in math once again. Although Ms. Davis was a fantastic teacher, she explained important concepts way too quickly for me. I was discouraged. And even though I was able to keep my head above water for a while because of Ms. Jacobson, I was now falling further behind than ever before. I went to extra help sessions and reviewed the week's material with my mother every Saturday morning, and yet nothing seemed to work. My father noticed that I was in poor spirits and decided to surprise me. One day after work, he came home with a brand new Lacrosse stick. It was a white proton power head on a black Maverick *Wonder Boy* shaft. I was over the moon; it was my first "real" Lacrosse stick.

Organized Lacrosse did not start in my township until fourth grade, but that did not mean I could not get a head start. I went to the back of our chimney with a Lacrosse ball and started learning how to play wall-ball. I played for a few hours and quickly realized that catching and throwing was much harder than I thought it would be. I dropped so many passes. My father came out and watched me struggle to catch and throw. He wanted to join in, so he picked up one of his old sticks and we started to have a catch. Immediately, I realized just how great he was at the sport. He was a wizard with his stick. My father taught me the fundamentals of the game, and we spent the rest of the night working on my technique. I truly began to understand how much he loved the game of Lacrosse as we finished our conversation and headed back inside.

My father often talked about how he loved being part of a team and how he continues to be best friends with many of his college teammates. I thought that if I became a college player, then surely I would have the same joy and happiness that he seemed to have. Right then and there, I decided that I wanted to be exactly like my father. I thought that playing college Lacrosse would make him proud of me. But, as my father said to me that night and still reminds me to this day, "everyone has their own path in life - don't follow my path - you need to find your own. Mom and I will always support you in whatever that is." And although I heard his words, I did not comprehend them at the time. I continued to believe that the only way to make my father proud was to play Division 1 Lacrosse. I sat in bed that night and began to manifest my dream. *I am going to play D1 Lacrosse. I am going to make my father proud of me.* I must have said it out loud at least thirty times — I would do anything to make my dream come true.

Summer crept back around, and I rejoined Carter on the Marple Newtown Tigers while also starting back up with Ms. Jacobson. In my free time, I went to the back of my chimney and played wall ball against it. I would spend hours in my backyard; the motion of catching and throwing became almost therapeutic for me. I was often discouraged by my right hand, but always knew that I could distract myself by improving my left-handed shot. As the summer went on, I began to see improvement and decided to transfer my hand-eye coordination skills over to the soccer field. I could not run as fast or change direction as quickly as everyone else, but I wanted to be part of a team.

At that age, not many kids wanted to play goalie - so I decided to switch positions and play goalie for the Tigers. It required the least amount of running and was the easiest way to hide my disability while on the field. During our games, I would always hug the right goalpost and just use my left side to cover a majority of the net. Surprisingly, my strategy worked well against most of the teams we played. My teammates always asked me why I did not stand in the middle of the net or try to block shots with my right hand, but eventually, I learned just to let their questions roll right off my back. Even though my strategy was not perfect, it got the job done. I was happy to be able to enjoy soccer and be part of a team despite my disability. I had found ways to compensate for my limp and lack of ability; I was proud of myself. I played against kids with zero disabilities week in and week out. And most of the time, I was able to hold my own.

Year Nine

I started my first day of third grade on September 9th, 2007. I was lucky enough to be placed in Mr. Hark's class with my friends Connor and Alex once again. On our first day, Mr. Hark introduced cursive and multiplication to us. The concepts went entirely over my head. I understood the rationale behind cursive handwriting, but could not even begin to understand multiplication. I had to schedule meetings with Mr. Hark after school, where he would explain the concepts in further detail. I always tried my hardest to understand and follow the steps that he laid out for me, but it was no use. I could not do more than three multiplication problems on my own. I was discouraged. I felt useless and defeated.

At the end of September, Mr. Hark introduced my peers and me to the "minute clinic." The minute clinic was a sheet of multiplication problems that our class would have to complete every Friday before he would allow us to go out to recess. We were supposed to finish the sheet in under a minute, but I never got more than halfway down the page. The top three fastest finishers, with the most right, of course, received a prize at the end of the day. By the second week of October, I found out just how demoralizing these minute clinics could be. They quickly became my worst nightmare. For some reason, I became extremely anxious every time Mr. Hark started his stopwatch. I began to develop a nervous habit of tapping my leg and gritting my teeth. It was stressful. I was never able to finish all of the problems in time and was one of a few students in my class who never even received a prize.

Reading had always come easily to me, but math felt like a foreign language. My mother tried her best to help. She would sit at the dinner table with me for hours after school and on weekends, I was not allowed to leave until we finished my homework in each subject. It proved to be a time for my mother and me to become closer, but we did not end up making that much progress. I had spent multiple summers in tutoring sessions with Ms. Jacobson, and yet it still took me twice as long as my friends to complete the multiplication version of the minute clinic. And although I was upset, my mother refused to give up. She forced me back to the dinner table and continued helping me every day. Eventually, my math skills improved, but never in timed situations.

    I spent the rest of the year continuing to practice Lacrosse and staying active. I hit the wall most days, but still ran into trouble when I tried to put the stick in my right hand. I could barely even hold the stick correctly; it always seemed to fall out. One day at the end of the fall, my father came out to watch me play wall ball and shoot on goal. He told me to put the stick in my right hand; he wanted to see what I could do. He scooped up a couple of balls from behind the net and began to throw me feeds. I made a nice cut towards the goal, but unfortunately missed every single pass he threw to me. I was distraught. Here I was, the son of a professional Lacrosse player, and I could not even catch a simple feed. I started to cry and threw my stick at the pitch back. I walked inside with tears streaming down my face. My father picked up my stick and ran to the back door so that he could hug me. He could see how upset I was, and always seemed to know how to make the situation better. "Ty... It is okay. Some of the best players in the world are Canadian. They only use one hand. They never use their off-hand. You can mold your game after them. It's all going to be okay." He told me not to worry and to just have fun playing the game.

    After dinner that night, my father told my mother about my breakdown. They talked about how they could help me and discussed whether or not I should pursue sports given my disability. Unbeknownst to me, this was a conversation that my mother and father would have multiple times in the years ahead. *Would there be too many disappointments in playing sports? Would it cause too much heartache?* My father would always tell me, "You don't have to play sports to be happy. Lots of kids - most kids - have a happy and healthy childhood and don't play any competitive sports." But I refused to listen. I told them that I loved sports. I told them that I loved being on a team and that I loved competing. And after many nights of discussions, they realized that this was truly what I wanted as they watched me shoot hoops, play wall ball, or talk about sports with my friends.

    With a lot of unease about the road ahead, my parents agreed to support my journey with sports. My mother suggested that maybe I should play a sport that only required one hand. That way, I would be able to excel with my left hand and would not have to worry as much about the various issues with my right side. My parents suggested I should give squash a try. I only agreed because I knew that it would make them happy. My father played a bit of squash with his friends and took me to Berwyn Squash and Fitness in hopes that I would enjoy playing with him. He was right, and so my parents decided to sign me up for squash lessons. And although I told my parents that I was happy to start playing a new sport, in reality, I was not. I never wanted to play an individual sport. I have always loved the camaraderie that comes with being part of a team. My dream was still to play Division I Lacrosse just like my father.

At Berwyn, I had my first ever squash lesson with their head professional, Luiz Sanchez, on a Thursday night after school. Luis was 5'6" and stocky, but unbelievably talented on the squash court. He had been hampered by leg injuries his entire professional career and was still able to top the national rankings. He taught me the fundamentals of the game: how to serve, how to hit a forehand, what shots qualified as "out," and where to stand. Secretly, my mother told Luis about my disability after I finished a lesson one day. He could not believe it. I did not notice at the time, but Luis started to treat me much differently than any of his other students. He was friendly and always forgiving. We began to develop a bond that lasted for the next three years.

I finished the school year and found myself playing for the Marple Newtown Tigers that summer once again. Soccer had pretty much taken a backseat to the other sports in my life, but I still enjoyed playing on the same team as Carter. Unfortunately, I was beaten out for the starting goalie spot and spent most of the season riding the bench. It started to upset me by the end of our third game. I hated sitting the bench—I wanted to be out there, I wanted to be on the field. It killed me to watch my teammates sub on and off the field while I never got the chance to play. It started to impact my mood, so I decided to focus more on other sports. I played Lacrosse more than I usually would and began playing more and more squash with my father. By the end of summer, I had come to accept that I was not going to have a future in the sport of soccer because of my disability. I would miss playing with Carter and my other teammates, but I could not overcome my deficit. I discussed all of this with my parents, and we agreed that I should stop playing soccer. It was time to move on.

Year Ten

My first day of fourth grade, September 13, 2008, was highlighted by change. That summer, Episcopal had moved from two split campuses, Devon and Merion, to one single campus in Newtown Square. Connor and I were placed in Ms. Sollenberger's class and were lucky enough to be able to experience all of these new amenities first hand. The Newtown Square campus had brand new facilities, modern classrooms, and most importantly, a brand new lower school turf field. My classmates and I played all different types of sports on the field during recess. Whether it was kickball, soccer, foursquare, or football, we did not care. We were just happy to be outside. Ms. Sollenberger, like Ms. Jacobson, tried her best to help me in math. By October, we had started to arrange weekly meetings. The meetings were not long in duration, but they ended up being beneficial. We would always discuss the upcoming week and plan out study sessions for each of my tests.

In December, my family and I made a significant change of our own. We moved to a different house on the other side of Newtown Square. My parents decided that a home in the neighborhood almost directly behind Episcopal's new campus was too attractive to pass up. When I heard the news, I was overcome with emotion. The move meant that I would no longer be living across the street from Carter, who had been my best friend for so many years. I did not want us to grow apart; I could not imagine losing the ability to walk over to his house every day after school. For the next couple of weeks, I became increasingly upset. I begged my parents to change their decision every single day. I even kicked the "For Sale" sign down and threw it in our trash can. Carter saw me move the sign from across the street and ran outside to see what I was doing. I hated having to tell him the news. Tears were streaming down my face as I went in to hug him, but he actually took the news well. He assured me that everything would be fine. "We are still friends, man... We'll never lose that." The day he saw the moving trucks pull up to my house, he wrote a note to our family and left it in the mailbox. The letter was attached to a drawing of my family moving into our new house, and Carter made sure to draw bright smiles across each of our faces.

The First Twenty

Two months later, my family and I moved in. The moving process was a hassle, but it ended up being a great decision. My parents were right. I had all of my friends over for a play-date a week after we settled in. We chased each other around the backyard and eventually discovered that my house was only a short walk to the fields at Episcopal. We grabbed a soccer ball and started on our way. Even though we had to climb across massive rocks and make our way through an empty lot, we did not care. It was a bonding experience for us, and we ended up playing hours of "World Cup" on Episcopal's turf field. I was comfortable in my new environment and, slowly but surely, started to fall in love with the new house. It began to feel like home.

That winter, I started playing for Episcopal's youth basketball team. All of my best friends immediately became my teammates, and I could not wait to play organized basketball. Mr. Jones, our head coach, decided not to hold tryouts that year because he could barely fill out a roster. It meant that my friends and I had automatically made the team. We were beyond excited. I loved dribbling the ball down the court and passing to my teammates, so naturally, I assumed the point guard position. Two other classmates also joined the team looking to play point guard, and eventually, I was moved to second string. I was not as skilled of a ball-handler as they were, and I had been beaten out for the spot. It killed me that I was not a member of the starting five. And though I was discouraged, I tried not to let it get to me. I loved being part of the team. I figured that I might not be the most talented, but I could always put forth more effort than the next guy. I gave it my all at every practice and began to immerse myself in the game.

Later that month, a classmate of ours told us that our basketball had been approved for a spot in the Malvern Youth Basketball League (MYBL) one day at lunch. The news meant that we would have a new schedule and, quite possibly, a completely different team. Two days later, Mr. Jones sent an email confirming the news and forwarded our parents the new schedule. Our team was going to play twelve games, with one every weekend until the playoffs started in mid-June. Mr. Jones's email was met with overwhelming support from parents. All of our classmates who were not able to participate during the winter wanted to play for this team. In total, thirty kids signed up even though there were only twenty spots on the roster. Our coaches could not play favorites, and so they decided to hold tryouts on Saturday, April 7, to solve the problem. My friends and I were fearful—the tryouts were the only thing we talked about for the entire month of March. We did not want to miss a chance to play in a league against all of the best teams in our area. I had been able to improve my skills on the basketball court little by little each day and felt confident about my shot at making the team. All of my best friends were trying out alongside me; I did not want to imagine what would happen if one of us were to get cut.

    I woke up at 7:30 AM on the morning of Saturday, April 7, with butterflies in my stomach. Today was finally the day. I stuffed an entire plate of scrambled eggs down my throat before grabbing my backpack from the downstairs closest. I was about to pack my only red pinnie and a pair of sneakers in my bag when my father yelled up to me from the garage. It was time to go. I got in the car and tried my best to calm down. As was the case with every tryout, my father would ask me if I wanted him to talk to the coach beforehand. He always wanted to let the coaches know that I had a right-sided weakness, but I never let him tell them. I did not want any pity; I did not want special treatment. I made him promise not to talk to the coaches because I was embarrassed and ashamed of my deficit. I did not want anyone to know that I was different. I looked out the window and tried to envision every possible scenario for these tryouts in my head. I thought I knew precisely how the tryout would go. Mr. Jones had been my coach the previous year, so I figured he would use our old practices as a foundation for these tryouts and only change one or two drills. Boy was I wrong.

    My father and I arrived at the tryout early so that I could stretch and warm-up. I walked onto the court as my father took a seat on the bleachers and began to talk to some of the other parents while Mr. Jones blew his opening whistle and called us into the huddle. He spoke for a while about the creation of this new team, stressed the importance of work ethic, and told us all to have fun. We broke the huddle, and suddenly, the tryout began. As we started to shoot, my nervousness from the car ride quickly turned into excitement. I had spent hours working on my game and could not wait to show Coach Jones just how much I had improved. I wanted to fight for a starting spot. We started the tryout with a jog to the baseline. *Uh Oh... What's this?* We never started practice this way. Coach Jones gathered all the players in a semicircle around the coaches.

The First Twenty

"We're going to switch things up. We are going to start with offensive drives to the basket. Watch me." He demonstrated the drill for us twice and split us up. "Three lines of twelve. One coach per line. Coach Shuster, you go there, Coach Roberts you're over here. And... Go!" He blew his whistle, and our team split up. I jumped in the back of Coach Shuster's line. Once it was my turn to go, I had to grab a ball and try to dribble past Coach Shuster on my way to the basket. If I was successful, I could finish the drill with a layup. It seemed straightforward, so I grabbed a bunch of my friends and forced them to join me at the back of Coach Shuster's line.

I found myself at the front of the line in no time. I picked up a ball from the rack and took a deep breath. I spun the ball in my hands a couple of times and started to drive to the hoop. I was not able to get more than two steps before Coach Shuster blew his whistle. He poked the ball out of my hands and stopped the drill. "Son... why are you using your left hand? This drill is for your right hand. Start again. Put it in your right hand this time and drive past me, okay?" He blew his whistle, starting the drill over again. I picked up another ball from the rack, spun it in my hands, and closed my eyes. Hiding my disability from my friends had always been a feasible task, until now. I had only practiced dribbling with my right hand once before. There was no way it could go well. I put the ball in my right hand and started my drive. This time, I did not get more than a step before I lost the ball. As I took my first dribble, I mishandled the ball on its way back up. It bounced away from me and toward the sideline. The kids in the line across from me started to laugh. I thought that I could dribble with my right hand when, in reality, it just looked like I was trying to "slap" the ball to the ground as hard as possible. I could feel everyone's eyes turn to me. I started to tear up. Coach Shuster blew his whistle. He called me over.

"Coach...Coach... I'm sorry."

He cut me off, "You still can't dribble with your off-hand?" I shook my head and stared at the ground in silence. "What is your name, son?"

I had to choke the words out. "Tyler Burt... I'm Tyler Burt." I told him. I picked up the ball and ran to the back of the line; I was distraught. Everything that I had worked for was taken away from me in a matter of seconds.

During the next water break, I sat on the bench and stared at the coaches. I was shocked at what had just transpired. I knew it right then and there; I had blown my shot. Coach Jones blew his whistle and had us run through three more drills before calling the tryouts for the day. I did not even try to redeem myself. I knew my fate had already been sealed. Many of the players packed up and started to leave, but I just sat back down on the bench and cried. My father ran over and immediately wrapped me in a bear hug. "It's okay... It's okay... Everything's okay. I promise. You don't have to play basketball. I was cut from my High School basketball team. I was no good at basketball." He tried his best to console me. The tears would not stop streaming down my face. An hour later, I dragged myself back to the car.

For the next month, I tried to remove anything connected to basketball from my daily routine. I seriously debated quitting sports and thought that I might just focus on academics instead. I did not see a future in sports—or at least not one where I would be seen as anything but a disappointment. Instead, I found comfort in playing video games and reading. I continued to see my friends at school every day, and thankfully, they never brought up the tryouts. Looking back, it was probably because they did not want to upset me. Coach Jones emailed our parents a week later and released the final roster. My name was not on the email, but every one of my best friends' was. They had all made the team. I congratulated them and tried my best to look happy, but it was difficult to fake my feelings. I found out earlier in the day that I was one of only six kids who had not been invited back to the second round of tryouts. I was crushed and struggled to handle the rejection. I did not want to imagine all of my best friends hanging out together at practices and games without me. It made me feel sick to my stomach and more alone than ever before.

Luckily, I moved on from my basketball experience and looked forward to my first season of organized Lacrosse. My father asked me after school one day if I wanted to try out for the Radnor Youth Lacrosse (RYL) team. One of the organizers of RYL, Peter Samson, approached my father two weeks before tryouts were scheduled to take place and asked if he would be our head coach. He agreed without hesitation.

He told our family one night over dinner and I, quite literally, jumped out of my seat. I could not wait for the opportunity to play for

The First Twenty

my father. He has always been my role model, and I thought him coaching my team would allow us to spend even more time together. I began to practice Lacrosse more frequently and tried to carry my stick with me throughout the day. At the time, it was the only thing that I cared about. The tryout day finally came and my father and I drove to Radnor High School early one Saturday morning. I had no idea what to expect. I got out of the car and warmed up near the sidelines while my father introduced himself to some of the other players and parents. Much to my dismay, I hardly recognized anyone because most of my new teammates attended Radnor Elementary School. I grew increasingly nervous; I thought they would hold a grudge toward me. I laced up my cleats and took a deep breath.

An hour and a half later, my father blew his whistle and signaled for the team to meet him at the faceoff circle. I listened to his closing speech and jogged off the field. The tryouts were over, and I actually did pretty well. I sat down on the bench and threw my helmet off. I was sweating bullets. Even with my father as the coach, I thought that I was skilled enough to make the team. I was one of only two lefties on attack and had played well in the scrimmage. I was glad these tryouts were not a repeat of what happened with basketball. My father waited a week before sending out emails and showing me the final roster. I ran my finger over the names until finally spotting my own. "LET'S GO!" I started running around the house in my boxers; I was over the moon. My father proceeded to show me our schedule for the year. I could not wait to get started!

Through this Radnor Lacrosse team, I met my friend Matt Freese. Matt had started at Episcopal in the same grade as me that year and was going to be the starting goalie for our team. He was a great kid and was fantastic in net for us. To be honest, I did not know him that well from school. He was in a different homeroom, and I had not hung out with him much at recess. I reached out to him after tryouts, and we slowly started to form a friendship. At the time, he and another classmate of mine, Maximo Moyer, were best friends. They played soccer together and were both exceptional students. My friends and I enjoyed playing sports with Matt and Maximo. They joined our friend group, and from that moment on, we started hanging out with them every weekend.

In my free time, I went back to taking lessons with Luis and quickly discovered how much smaller a squash court is than a Lacrosse field or basketball court. It was infinitely easier to hide my disability. I only had to take three steps to get to any corner of the court and conditioned my left leg to support most of my weight. I brought over my right ankle brace from Lacrosse to prevent any injuries and re-tied my squash shoes with hockey laces. Hockey laces are probably three times tighter than the average shoelace, so I used them to fully secure my ankle. Not only did the laces end up accomplishing their primary goal, and they also somehow decreased the severity of my limp on court. And even though I was not able to move around perfectly, it was good enough. I improved my racket skills over the next few months and found squash to be more and more fun. The sheer competitiveness, matched with the size of the court, helped me forget about my disability.

I spent the spring playing my first season of organized Lacrosse. I started the season at the "X" position, but was moved to left attack by the end of our first game. The season flew by, and honestly, I loved playing for my father. He made Lacrosse interesting and exciting. Even though he never showed me any favoritism, he would make sure that I was happy and always tried his best to keep me from getting injured. Throughout the season, I grew closer with all of my teammates. I was shocked at the fact that they did not care that Matt and I went to Episcopal instead of Radnor. If we could produce on the field, then we were accepted and loved by the guys. I played the second half of the season at the left attack position and on the crease during man-up. I did not get many touches, but it did not really matter. I scored a goal in our playoff elimination game against BYC that year, and I was thrilled. It was an exciting moment in my life.

As I continued training with Luis weekly, I could not wait for the end of the school year. I started up with Ms. Jacobson the day after school ended and spent the rest of my free time playing wall ball. I picked my Lacrosse stick up and would beg my father to shoot with me every night. Eventually, I started forcing myself to make the ten to fifteen-minute walk to Episcopal's turf field whenever I wanted to play. For the rest of the summer, we went on several family vacations. I loved seeing my cousins and playing sports with them. On one occasion, my parents surprised my siblings and me with a trip to Pittsburgh. We pulled up to a dog breeder, and my mother told

The First Twenty

Caroline and me that we would be leaving that day with a Goldendoodle puppy. It was the most exciting news of the summer. Caroline, Wills, and I got out of the car and sprinted into the house. We were immediately greeted with ten Goldendoodle puppies; it felt like a dream. My siblings and I had the chance to pet the puppies for almost an hour while my mother weighed our options. We were finally able to agree on a young and energetic male puppy. My father put him in the passenger seat of our car and decided that we would call the dog "Dog X" until we came up with a more suitable name. Both Caroline and my mother suggested that we name the dog Lucky, but the rest of our family quickly vetoed it. "I mean, we are from Philly; so why not name the dog Rocky?" I blurted out as we pulled into our neighborhood. My whole family agreed, they thought the name was perfect. Rocky came home with us and slowly adapted to his new environment. Despite chewing through all of our shoes and moldings, we loved him anyway. Once summer ended, I could not even begin to imagine our lives without him.

Year Eleven

I started my first day of fifth grade on September 12, 2009. That year, Alex and I were placed in Mr. Levine's class while the rest of our friend group was across the hall with Mr. Powell. My friends and I changed floors and changed teachers, but everything else seemed to stay the same. And though the material was not as difficult as I had anticipated, I fell behind and consistently earned B to C grades on my tests. I had to set up after school meetings with Mr. Levine. As a result, I found myself "locked" in the classroom more than ever before and decided again to turn to sports as an outlet. To me, playing different sports became almost therapeutic. They helped me calm down and allowed me to have fun. I threw myself into the sport of squash and spent hours on the court, finding a work-around for each of my weaknesses. I continued this same routine almost exactly until January 10, which was one of the scariest days of my life.

On January 10, I experienced something that changed my life forever. The day started as normal as any other day. I ate a bowl of Cinnamon Toast Crunch for breakfast and went to Berwyn for my 10 AM lesson. Mrs. G dropped Connor at my house later that afternoon, and we played football and basketball for hours before deciding to attend that evening's "ice party" hosted by Episcopal at the Skatium Ice Arena. I was skeptical at first, but Connor eventually persuaded our entire friend group to go. I did not want to be left out. It was the first time I, or any of my friends, had attended one of these events. We had no idea what to think. The party was supposed to be a place for us to dance, skate, and meet girls away from our parents. What was not to like?

My friend group and I arrived at the Skatium at 7 PM, exactly when the party was scheduled to start. As Connor and I stepped out of the car, we were mesmerized by the loud music and the flashing lights. "Pocketful of Sunshine" by Natasha Bedingfield shook the building; it was evident that the party had already started. My friends and I checked out skates and began to enjoy ourselves. We raced each other around the ice for an hour and a half before going to the upstairs portion of the party to dance with the rest of our classmates. We

The First Twenty

danced and laughed at each other for a while until my father called to pick us up. I got off the phone with him and invited my entire friend group over for the night. I thought that we were all going to sleep in the basement together, but Connor ended up being the only friend to accept my invitation. My father arrived at the Skatium and he hurried us into the car. He wanted to get home as quickly as possible. After all, it was very late at night.

We spent the ride back to the house telling my father about the party, what girls we liked, and what dance moves we tried. As we arrived home and immediately ran upstairs, I realized that Connor did not want to sleep in our guest room. It was cold, and we both thought that the room was haunted. He asked for a sleeping bag, and I returned twenty minutes later with the only one in the house. I threw it on the ground and gave him a pillow. "Goodnight bro," I said as I jumped on my bed and closed my eyes. It was the last thing I remember.

I woke up in the back of a car three hours later. My family surrounded me, their eyes wet with tears. I started to scratch my face. "Guys... What is going on? Why are we in the car?" My mother shrieked a sigh of relief. "He's okay. T, he's okay. Thank God!" She wrapped me in a big hug. I looked around and tried to become familiar with my surroundings. My father was driving, and I was in the backseat of my mother's car with the rest of my family. *But what had happened?* I was so confused. I started to tap my fingers on the seat in front of me and looked up. Every member of my family had their eyes locked on me.

"What is going on? What happened? Why are we in the car?" I had so many questions, but none of them were answered. When we arrived at the Children's Hospital of Philadelphia, usually a 30-minute drive from my house, I was even more confused. My father swiftly picked me up and took me through the doors of the Emergency Room. His eyes were full of tears. *Oh no, what had I done now?* I thought. My father gave me to a doctor, who would later introduce himself as Dr. Leibowitz, and rushed back out the front door to get the rest of my family. Dr. Leibowitz laid me down on a hospital bed and began running tests. I grabbed his arm. "Excuse me, sir - what happened? Why am I here?"

He looked apologetic as he started to speak. "Tyler... your parents brought you here because they think you may have had a seizure a little while ago. Just try to relax. I am going to run some tests to make sure you're okay. Take some deep breaths."

I fell silent. *A seizure? A seizure? What even was a seizure?*

Dr. Leibowitz brought my family in from the hallway. "Doc, how is he? Is he going to be okay? What should we do?" They burst through the doors and into the room. My mother was thrilled to see that I was okay. A nurse began by taking my blood pressure and then performed a series of tests on me.

Dr. Leibowitz called the room to attention. "Mr. and Mrs. Burt, I am happy to say that your son is stable. Unfortunately, Tyler suffered a grand mal seizure last night. As of this moment, we still do not know why this happened, but we assure you we are doing everything in our power to make sure that he is okay. Nurses, help me." I started to tear up; I was terrified. *What does that mean?* He propped me up against the bed's headboard and took a stethoscope to my heart. "He'll be okay. Looks normal."

My mother squeezed my hand, "Don't worry. We got you. We love you." Dr. Leibowitz left the room and instructed his team to run another cycle of tests on me.

A half-hour later, he re-entered the room. "Tyler, you're gonna be okay." The tension in the room felt like it had been cut by a knife. Dr. Leibowitz walked over to my mother. "Tyler's gonna be fine. The cause of his seizure was likely dehydration from all of the skating, the bright lights and a lack of sleep. These things, combined with his past brain injury, caused his brain to have a hiccup.' My father sighed in relief. 'He's never had a seizure before, and his CT scan came back uneventful. We are almost positive it was dehydration, but we cannot be sure." He shook my hand and sat down at the foot of my bed. "Let's get you out of here." He left the room and told his nurses to wrap it up. I had a migraine headache, but the doctors said it was a common side effect of my seizure. Even though I was scared to leave the hospital, the medical team assured me that I was going to be okay. My parents believed them, so we got in the car and drove home. We arrived back at the house a little after 10 AM; I went straight to my room and right to bed.

The First Twenty

I spent the rest of my fifth-grade year terrified to fall asleep every night. I was not sure if I was going to wake up the next morning in my bed or in a car on the way to the hospital, it was genuinely petrifying. I tried to occupy my thoughts with sports and school, but it was no use. I did not feel like myself. It felt almost like I had "blacked out." I hardly remembered anything. Needless to say, I never went to another ice party ever again. I started improving my diet and forcing myself to drink more water. I distracted myself with every sport imaginable and tried to block the nightmares from entering my thoughts. Unfortunately, it did not always work. It was a horrible experience, but I leaned on my parents for support. They reassured me and helped me learn how to talk about my problems out loud. I used them to escape my depression. After a couple of weeks, I slowly started feeling like myself. My mood improved, and I began to smile again.

At the start of spring, I begged my parents to try out for my first ever travel Lacrosse team. Named the "Philly Fever" Lacrosse club, this team would be comprised of some of the best players from our area. I was unbelievably excited; I could not wait to finally play on the same side as all of my friends. I was still going to play for my father on the township team that upcoming spring, but hoped to make this travel team for the summer. Tryouts were in March. I talked about the team in school and discovered that Luke, Matt, and I were all going to try out. If we made the final roster, we would be competing in three summer tournaments against the best travel teams in the country. It was nerve-racking, but equally exciting at the same time.

Tryouts came more quickly than expected. On the morning of March 9, my father woke me up and drove me to the Haverford School. I tried to sleep in the car, but I was too amped up. I could not wait to finally play on the same team as my best friends. When we arrived at Haverford, I got out of the car, grabbed my gear, and said goodbye to my father. This time he would not be coaching me. I met some of my new teammates in the parking lot, and we jogged down to the grass field. As soon as I threw my bag on the sideline, one of the coaches blew their whistle and told us to meet him at the center of the field. Our head coaches gathered us in a semi-circle around the faceoff 'X' and introduced us to John Nostrant, the head of Fever Lacrosse Club. He was intimidating. I fell silent and jogged to the sideline with my head down. I was unbelievably nervous; I wanted to make the team more than ever. All of the best players from my area and some of my best friends were grouped together and standing on the sideline with me. I prayed that no one would notice my disability.

    In the tryouts, I actually played well, but was not convinced that it was enough for me to make the team. Although all of the players at the tryouts could run faster than me, at least my lefty shot was pretty decent. By the time we finished tryouts, I was discouraged by my performance on the field. I did not talk the entire ride home. Thankfully, my father came to my aid. He gave me a hug when we got out of the car and sat me down in the living room. He told me how he had gotten cut from his high school basketball team in his junior year and did his best to comfort me. "It's okay. It's okay." He said. "If this is what YOU want and you don't make it, use it as fuel. Let your disappointment be the reason why you want to go out and get better every single day. You got this." He brought tears to my eyes. He was there for me and helped me prepare for the possibility of disappointment. I will always be grateful; he made me realize that giving up does not have to be an option.

    Two weeks later, Matt and Luke were over my house for a play-date when one of the head coaches emailed our parents a copy of the final roster. My mother called us to the computer, but I was too scared to look at the screen. I hid in the bathroom as Matt and Luke violently refreshed the page. Suddenly, they started screaming. Matt ran over and hugged me. "Tyler! Tyler! We all made the team. Let's go!" I jumped in the air and celebrated. I genuinely could not believe it; I had made the team. Matt, Luke, and I started a mosh pit and ran around the house with our shirts off. It was hilarious. We could not contain our excitement. I ran to the living room and hugged my father. I was so fired up!

    I spent the rest of the spring playing for my township Lacrosse team and trying not to fall behind in the classroom. For the most part, I was able to keep up with my work because of Mr. Levine. He was never too busy for my questions and also helped strengthen my organizational skills in our after school meetings. I continued to struggle in math, specifically with fractions, but he was always willing to lend a helping hand. I used the rest of the spring to get back on the squash court and prepared myself for summer Lacrosse. I blinked, and suddenly, I was moving into middle school.

The First Twenty

As the summer started, my family and I fell into our normal summer routine and began visiting family members along the East Coast. We slept at home for only a night or two before driving to South Jersey to visit Uncle Doug and his family. We attended a family barbeque, swam in their pool, and played volleyball for hours. It was a wonderful time with family. When we finally came home, I got back into squash and Lacrosse. I would go out to the backyard with a bucket of balls and shoot until it was dark. I tried playing wall ball and switching to my right hand but had little success. I could not get enough power behind my shot because of my disability. Yes, I was physically able to shoot it, but that did not mean that it was a "good" shot. Even though it was demoralizing, I was confident that I could find ways to circumnavigate my disability. I continued playing Lacrosse and found myself constantly returning to Berwyn. I tried to spend my time soloing or in lessons with Luis.

For practice, I would hit 100 forehands, 100 backhands, 100 volleys, 100 drop-shots, and 100 cross courts. It was tedious, and yet I forced myself to stick with it. A few weeks after I had started this routine, Luis informed my family and me that he would be taking a job in Chicago. He had been offered better pay and a more prestigious squash professional job at one of the major racket clubs of Chicago. I was sad to see him go, but I knew it was the right decision for him and his family. He was an unbelievable coach and the reason why I started playing the game competitively. I'll always be grateful to him.

I spent the rest of the summer playing for Fever LC and trying to find a new squash club. My mother often had to enlist Aunt Carrie's help to get my siblings and me to the right place at the right time. I enjoyed practices and workouts with Fever, but often found myself riding the benching tournament games. Even though it did not bother me at first, the bad thoughts eventually started to come in waves. I wanted to be on the field. I wanted to be part of the action. I often watched from the sidelines as my friends and teammates played in unbelievably competitive games during our three tournaments. I played in small amounts throughout every tournament, but rarely in the big games or during important possessions. I was upset, and yet there was nothing I could do about it. My father was not the coach; he could not just sub me in. For the rest of the summer, I supported my teammates from the sidelines and tried to take advantage as my opportunities slowly arose. I continued to practice my stick skills and eventually broke through. In our last tournament, I put up a couple of points. I was excited and bitter at the same time. I wished my shot had come earlier that summer; maybe I could've impacted a game and turned one of our losses into a win.

I finished the season and was preparing to go back to school when my mother and I received a call about the Fairmount Athletic Club. They were in the process of starting a training program, "The Scozzie Squash Academy" and wanted to gauge my parent's interest. With Luis moving to Chicago, my parents decided to join the club. We dropped Berwyn and signed up for The Scozzie Squash Academy instead. My mother and I arrived at Fairmount for my first ever session a week later. Paul and Lyall were the head squash professionals at Fairmount and the founders of Scozzie. Even though I was not a great player, they took me in and have treated me like family from the beginning. I started training with other juniors from around the area and grew excited about the future of Scozzie's program.

Scozzie's training is unique because we always played every drill with a match play component. The losers of each drill have to move to a lower court, and the winners move to the higher court. I hated losing, I never wanted to move down a court and play with less-skilled players. The match-play component always motivated me to get better. And as Paul and Lyall started to work with me more often, they introduced me to US Squash and Junior Tournaments. I started my US Squash career by playing Bronze tournaments at various clubs scattered throughout Philadelphia. I never actually played well in any of my matches, but they allowed me to gain match-play experience. I began to really enjoy Scozzie and started spending more of my time with my coaches both on and off the court. We formed a real friendship, and my mother eventually told them about my disability. I thought that they would discourage me from coming and playing at the club, but they ended up doing the exact opposite. They were amazed at the obstacles I had overcome and wanted to do everything they could to help me succeed. To this day, I am so grateful for their support.

BOOK IV

THE MIDDLE SCHOOL

YEARS

(8/10/2010)

Year Twelve

I started my first day of sixth grade on September 9, 2010. As I walked through the two-tone "MIDDLE SCHOOL" doors for the first time, I realized that my life was going to change. The registrar assigned me a locker, placed me in different classes, and gave me a homeroom advisor. I was happy to gain independence, but realized soon after that it would come at a cost. After only a month in the classroom, I found myself looking to sports as my escape. Episcopal makes each of its students play three sports every year, so my friends and I decided to try out for the football team. Much to our dismay, we were immediately placed on the "B" team with the other sixth graders. We were disappointed, but came to understand that most of the schools in our league would not let a sixth-grader play on the "A" team.

My friends and I spent the next couple of days running footwork drills and working out for our new coaches. I had always wanted to play Quarterback, but unfortunately was moved to half-back a week after the tryouts ended. The move shook my confidence. I wanted to play Quarterback because I thought I had the best arm on the team. That, combined with the fact that I am a lefty, should have made the QB position mine. I was wrong; it did not. I was beat out for the spot and regularly found myself sitting the bench in practices and in games as our third string RB. I hated it. I began to overthink everything and got lost in my head. I found it difficult to celebrate my friends' playing time when I knew that I was not going to get any. My confidence was already fragile, and this made it worse. I could not understand why the coaches barely gave me the chance to play. I sat on the sidelines and cursed at myself day after day. The excuses started in the form of thoughts and eventually came out as "chirps" to verbally assault the other team. *I (You) should have just played Lacrosse, I (You) should have just stayed home, I (You) should have just been better in the tryouts. I (You) suck.* The nightmares came back, and I regularly spent nights awake. I stared at the ceiling for hours. I felt depressed; it was awful. Looking back, I realize that even though I hated Football that year, it taught me some pretty good life lessons. It began to teach me how to accept responsibility, how to put your head down and grind, and,

The First Twenty

perhaps most importantly, how to deal with disappointment once again.

I finished out the season and could not wait to step back on the squash court. I played in my first ever US Squash sanctioned Junior Silver tournament just two days before Episcopal's school tryouts. I entered the tournament and thought that I was ready to make the jump up to better competition, but I was wrong. I was knocked out in the first round. My opponent came out quickly and easily defeated me. He moved to the ball effortlessly and seemed to know exactly where I was going with every shot. I tried my hardest, but it was just not enough. I felt like I was stuck in quicksand; my opponent effectively moved me around the court and capitalized on my mistakes. It was embarrassing. I lost the match and was so upset at myself that I forced my mother to drive me all the way to Scozzie right after we finished. I was now hungrier than ever. I hated the fact that my opponent had to take it easy on me—that he almost had to give me points. I had always hated losing, but this one felt different. This one physically hurt.

I returned to training and looked forward to the start of a new season. I thought that I would have time to focus on squash, but almost immediately found myself being ushered into tryouts for my travel Lacrosse team. The last Saturday in November, Fever LC held open tryouts to decide on the tournament team for the upcoming summer. I was happy to strap on my helmet and pads; I could not wait to play with my best friends again. Much to my surprise, everyone from the previous year came back to re-tryout for the team. My father and I arrived at the tryout early to stretch and warm-up. We could not believe how popular Fever LC had become. I looked down and saw thirty new players crowding the sideline. *That cannot be for our tryouts . . . Can it?* At least sixty kids were trying out for only 30 spots, and I quickly realized that the tryouts were going to get very competitive.

All things considered, I blocked out the negative thoughts and performed pretty well. I had a goal in the scrimmage and added two goals and an assist in the man-up drills. I was excited and full of energy as our coaches blew their whistles and signaled for our first water break, but unfortunately, it all went downhill from there. The coaches made us run one-on-one drills for the rest of the tryout. My defenders almost immediately realized that I could not carry the ball with my right hand. They began positioning themselves to stop any movement to my left side and keyed in on my weakness. Pretty quickly, every defender began dominating our matchup. I ended the tryout going 0 / 6 in shots on goal, and yet still had a difficult time believing that I would get cut from the team. *So I am not a one on one guy, who cares?* I thought. I knew that I could be useful on man-up or in transition, I just needed a shot.

    I left the tryouts that day and began to prepare for my first season of organized squash. I started training three to four times a week and specifically tried to build up my cardio. I told myself every day that I was not going to suffer another disappointing tournament loss and promised myself that I would tirelessly to make sure that I won. I spent time on the stationary bike, on the VersaClimber, and ghosting to different corners of the court. For school tryouts, our coaches evaluated us by making us play round-robins with each other. As a sixth-grader, I was told that my classmates and I had to start from the bottom of the ladder. No favoritism, you play for your spot. Exactly the way it should always be done. Eventually, I cemented myself as a member of the "B" team and won enough matches to switch between #4 and #5 on the ladder that season.

    At the time, I was still playing squash for fun. I loved to compete and I also loved to win, but mainly used the sport as a workout for Lacrosse. I wanted to play Division 1 Lacrosse more than anything in the world; it was all I talked about. I genuinely believed that my father would be more proud of me if I played college Lacrosse. I did not know as much as I do now. I did not understand that my father has always been proud of me, right from the moment I was born. He is astonished by my progress—not only in athletics, but also in life. He has told me numerous times that I "should not measure myself by Lacrosse or by any other sport." But I never used to listen. I did not understand that he loved me for me, regardless of my accomplishments and despite my disability. In my immature brain, I thought Lacrosse was going to be the only way to make him proud.

    I returned home from squash practice one day to gut-wrenching news. I started to cry as I found out that I had been cut from the upcoming summer's Fever team. My name was not among those on the final roster when the coaches emailed my parents earlier that morning. Two of the coaches called my father to express their condolences. At the end of the conversation, they asked if I would have any interest in playing for the Fever "B" team. They wanted me to play and asked if my father would coach. I was speechless; I could not even fathom the thought of playing for another team. I sprinted to my room and locked the door. I could not believe that all of my friends were going to play on the "A" team without me. I felt left out. I wedged myself in a corner and did not stop crying until my pillow was soaked with tears. I was heartbroken. I was angry and started to make brash decisions. I cursed God, shouted at my parents, and tried to punch holes in my wall. It was bad. I hated myself. I could not understand why God cursed me with this disability. I felt like my stroke had taken away all of my athletic potential.

It was weeks before I wanted to get back on the squash court. I started training at Scozzie again and ended the school season with a record of five wins and three losses. It was not the way I wanted to end my first season, but the losses gave me the motivation to go back to training every day. To end the season, I entered two Junior Silver tournaments. The first was in Philadelphia and the second in North Jersey. Even though I played reasonably well in both of the tournaments, I was unable to make it past the quarterfinals. Both of the opponents that I had lost to were much more technically skilled than I was, and ended up beating me effortlessly (3 – 0), (3 - 0).

The winter season ended, and I exchanged my squash racket for a Lacrosse stick. I prepared to tryout out for the Middle School Lacrosse team and was excited to play another season of township Lacrosse. Much to my disappointment, RYL called my father two weeks before the scheduled tryouts and told my father that we could no longer be a part of Radnor Lacrosse. We did not live in Radnor Township (even though my parents once owned a Lacrosse store in Wayne) and the members of the youth athletic board were no longer willing to "grandfather" me in. They wanted me to play for Conestoga or Marple Newtown, the two districts that my house lies between. My father called the head of Conestoga Youth Lacrosse (CYL) the next day to try and fix the issue. Thankfully, it worked. We were immediately accepted into the Conestoga family and, just like that, I was a member of CYL.

Youth Lacrosse tryouts ended up being tremendously different than school Lacrosse tryouts. All of the sixth graders were immediately placed on the "B" team once again, while the "A" team was comprised of the best seventh and eighth-graders.

Once the teams were split up, we were all allowed to compete for a starting spot. My ankle brace raised some questions almost immediately. The coaches started to question why I could not carry the ball to my right side and why my balance looked off. I was afraid to tell them about my stroke and decided to keep it a secret. I brushed the questions off as best I could and blamed my mistakes on a lack of practice. Despite my ankle, I promised the coaches that I would work as hard as possible to get better. I played as best I could for the "B" team. I made some accurate feeds and could always score with my left hand. I was not helpless; instead, I felt like I was being held back. I was a good player, but my disability held me back from being great. One of my classmates beat me out for the starting lefty attack spot, so I found myself sitting on the bench once again. I sat and watched from the sidelines as my friends were inserted into the starting lineup. I tried to support them as best I could. I cheered when any of my teammates scored a goal and would always high five my friends after we broke the huddle. I tried incredibly hard to cover up my disappointment. As I sat on the sidelines, I promised myself that I was going to get better. I promised myself that I was going to be in the starting lineup next year. I was going to do everything in my power to make that promise a reality.

Later that spring, I received some news after a routine visit with Dr. Whoeling. She informed my mother and me that I was not growing and thought that I might have a pituitary gland deficiency. She wanted to explore options for treatment. I was just under the 5th percentile in height for my age group, and Dr. Whoeling suggested that I see a Human Growth Hormone (HGH) specialist as a possible solution. I was speechless when my mother explained the news to me. I knew that I had not hit puberty yet, but I always just figured that I would grow eventually. My father is 6'0," and my mother is 5'4", so I thought that I was going to be okay. Boy was I wrong! I checked into the lab two floors beneath the doctor's office and spent six hours hooked up to an IV while the doctors ran various tests on me. With no other means of entertainment, I watched movies to take my mind off of the testing. It proved to be a painstakingly long process, and I spent the majority of my day praying for the tests to be over. The tests confirmed what was

The First Twenty

suspected, I was growth hormone deficient, and I would have to begin self-administering daily shots. It was upsetting. I hated that I would have to begin self-administering daily shots. It was another reminder that I was different, but at least I would begin growing and getting stronger.

I finished the school year and was ecstatic to discover that my summer was going to be much less hectic than the end of my school year. I put my down my Lacrosse stick and picked up my squash racket. I was not playing any summer Lacrosse, so I used my free time training at Scozzie. I started regularly attending their training sessions once again and loved connecting with my coaches. My mother decided to sign me up for three tournaments that summer. I could not wait for Scozzie, and especially Paul, to coach me in action. "I played in two Silver tournaments and one Gold tournament that summer, but unfortunately, did not achieve my desired results in any of them. I always let my immaturity get the best of me. I never made it past the semi-finals of any of the Silvers and was knocked out in the first round at the University of Virginia Gold. I played in the UVA Gold to end the summer, and upon losing that match, I almost broke my racket out of frustration. I was miserable the entire ride back from Virginia. My mother pulled over the car when we were just five minutes away from the house; she had seen enough. I only cared about myself and did not show any respect for my opponent or coaches. She wouldn't put up with it. She could not believe that I had shown such poor sportsmanship. And although I was initially upset at her, I ended up coming to my senses. I apologized and promised to change my behavior on court.

Year Thirteen

I started my first day of seventh grade on September 18, 2011. I walked into class on the first day and was relieved to be familiar with the middle school and its various challenges. The workload increased even more, and it honestly took a while for me to adjust. I had to lean on my parents and most of my friends for help with algebra and non-fiction book reports. That year, seventh grade, was the first year that I started to branch out and tried talking to girls. I researched one-liners and used my friends for practice. Regrettably, it never went well. I often stuttered from nervousness and could never take my eyes off of the floor. I thought that talking to girls would be a piece of cake—I was a happy and energetic kid who could never keep his mouth shut. It should have been easy, but it was not. I was scared to admit that I lacked any real confidence. I could barely get a word out when I talked to any girl; it was downright embarrassing. Deep down, I think it was because I was terrified of anyone, let alone a girl, finding out about my stroke. I did not want anyone to know my secret I wanted people to think that I was normal. I was always scared that girls would treat me differently. I felt like I was never good enough; I thought that I was a disappointment.

That fall, I was denied enough times that I found myself going back to the cold, dark corners of my thoughts. I cried in my room almost every night. I began feeling like I was "less than human" and questioned how I would ever find a girlfriend. My depression started to kick in I had convinced myself that any girl would leave me upon learning that I was disabled. One time, I even had a nightmare of a girl leaving me for one of my best friends. It was awful. The thoughts came in waves, and some days, I could not get out of bed. Luckily, my family and friends came to my aid. Even though I shut them out, they helped me in ways that I cannot even begin to explain. Eventually, they helped get me back to the energetic and happy kid that I had always been.

I fell right back into my daily routine just in time for the last day of football tryouts. I met with the coach before practice and asked for a chance to try out for the team. I was embarrassed about my HGH issue, so I decided to tell him that I had missed the entire week because of the

The First Twenty

flu virus. He did not believe me, and yet somehow still allowed me to try out for the "A" team the next day. It was a miracle, considering I did not have a written doctor's note. A half-hour later, I took the field with my teammates. I was ready, but unfortunately, I did not perform nearly as well as I could have. I missed passes, I missed blocks, and I missed tackles. Basically, I missed everything. It was humiliating. I was one of only a handful of seventh-graders cut from the "A" team that year. I had to pretend to be happy for my friends who made the team, but found it increasingly difficult to mask my disappointment.

As the season continued, I started to earn playing time as a slot receiver for the "B" team. I caught almost every ball thrown to me one day in practice, and so the coaches put me in the slot for a game. I did not do much, but we had not thrown a pass all season, so I knew what to expect. I was on the field either to be a blocker or a distraction on every play. I used my left side as my anchor and tried to direct any hits to my left shoulder. My right side was weak and had to act almost like a backup, while my left side became the foundation for all of my athletic success. And because I was constantly using my side, my mother began to notice that I was developing a difference in my muscle tone. My right side was shrinking, while my left side was only getting bigger. I needed to get back into PT.

When Football season ended, I picked my squash racket back up and returned to Scozzie. I started training four days a week in preparation for school tryouts and could not wait to start taking lessons from Paul again. I worked tirelessly to improve my deep backhand and forehand drop shot. I spent day after day at Fairmount, and eventually, my hard work started to pay off. I won some matches and was moved up to the #7 position on my school team. As soon as the tryouts ended, I went back to the locker room and screamed in excitement. *I had finally made an "A" team!* It felt amazing.

That winter, I decided to take a break from Junior tournaments and just play for our school team. I was one of only two seventh graders to make the "A" team; and I was happy. I could not wait for the season to start. I wanted to prove to myself that I could be just as good as my teammates despite my disability. I played out the season in the #7 position. And though I ended with a record of 4 - 1 in the Inter-Ac, I blew a 2 - 1 lead to Clayton King and Conestoga in our final match of the year. I was embarrassed when I walked off the court and tried apologizing to my teammates and coaches. I froze up—I was not ready for the spotlight. I lacked any confidence when playing in important matches. I did not have any real experience yet, and I did not know how to close a game out. I played disastrously; Clayton knew that I had lost my head. He took the lead in the fifth and never looked back. I lost the fifth game 11-3, and with that, my teammates and I also lost the match. I could not even begin to explain what had gone wrong; I kicked myself the entire ride home and tried to forget about squash for the rest of the winter. I could not wait for the season to come to an end.

I spent the spring playing Lacrosse for both CYL and Episcopal. Sadly, I did not play well for either team that season. I had no confidence on the field, and it took less than a quarter for most of my defenders to realize it. They took advantage of me because I could not carry to my right hand and because I was undersized. I was tough and took a beating from defensemen, but realized that my disability was impacting my performance more and more. For a few weeks, I struggled to find my place on the team. I could not play right Attack because of my disability, and I was not fast enough to beat anyone on a dodge coming from X, so my coaches decided to move me to the crease. From then on, I surprised everyone and put together a productive half of the season. I was thrilled to find a position where I could have success!

I was so happy with the way the season had ended that I decided to take another stab at summer Lacrosse. Only this time, I tried out for NXT LC instead of Fever. I could not take a second rejection from Fever, so I knew that I had to try out for another club. I wanted a fresh start and ended up making the NXT team after two rounds of tryouts. I got to know my new teammates and spent the summer splitting time at the crease attack position. I scored most of my goals on man-up and ended the season with a few goals and several assists. I thanked my coaches after our last tournament over and over again—I was elated with the way that I had finished the summer. I was able to prove to myself that I could contribute to the success of a team despite my disability. I was paving my own way, and it felt good.

As I gained more confidence, I began to feel more comfortable on the Lacrosse field as well as on the squash court. I spent most of my free time at Fairmount working to improve my game. I set up matches with anyone who lingered around the courts and rarely declined a challenger. August slowly turned to September, and I started to see progress in not only my technique, but also in my movement. I had found ways to compensate for my disability without even realizing it. I was ecstatic about my progress and could not wait to get back on court for Episcopal. I spent the rest of my summer at home or on the beach hanging with friends and preparing for the start of my eighth-grade year.

Year Fourteen

I started my first day of eighth grade on September 12, 2012. I was content to find out that not much within the middle school had changed, except for the fact that we were now the oldest kids in the building. My friends and I thought we "ran" the school. Almost immediately, I grew comfortable with my new class schedule and most of my teachers. And though the workload was more significant once again, I figured out ways to compensate. I tried out for football and finally made the "A" team. It felt great. Although I did not contribute much, I worked as hard as I possibly could and came to practice every day with a positive attitude. In most of our games, I sat on the sidelines and continued to envy all of the great athletes around me.

I was lucky enough to find peace on the squash court. My soloing sessions became therapeutic and soothing. I began to feel like the squash court was the only place in the world where I could tune out everyone else and just be myself. It was a place where I could work to better myself and my own game. I trained at Scozzie for a couple of weeks, and before I knew it, I was in the midst of tryouts once again. I entered school tryouts eager for the chance to play in Inter-Ac matches and ready to take on more responsibility within the team. I ended the tryouts as the #3 ranked player on the ladder and played out the season. Surprisingly, I actually played reasonably well. I ended the year with a winning record and won my biggest match of the season.

Once I finished the winter season, I started playing Lacrosse right away. I tried out for Episcopal and was psyched to finally make the "A" team. I could not wait to take the field and play alongside my best friends. I was glad when I found out that the tryouts were going to be almost exactly the same as the year before. Only this time, I was going to be ready. I knew what to expect. At the end of the week, I actually turned in a few good practices and was beyond excited when our coaches announced that I would be one of the starting attackmen for our first game. I was quickly able to find my niche on man-up and played well from the crease. The season flew by, and my mood improved drastically with each game. I was more excited than ever to take the field with my teammates and started to have fun playing the sport of Lacrosse again.

Towards the end of the season, my limp started to get worse. While measuring both of my feet, my orthopedic doctor was shocked to discover that I was beginning to develop a leg length discrepancy. My left leg was 1.5 inches longer than my right leg. Regrettably, the doctor went on to inform me that I was possibly going to need surgery to correct this issue. She stringently told me to continue with PT and daily stretching. Hopefully, a combination of those two things would ward off surgery.

Unfortunately for me, the bad news did not end there. Finals eventually came around, and I struggled to memorize all of the information. My mother re-hired a tutor for the week leading up to my exams, but it was still not enough. I was too immature and not ready to take on the responsibility of a high school student. I approached my parents and asked if I could visit a neighboring all-boys school, The Haverford School. Although they were our rivals, I had friends at the school and wanted to find out more about it. I visited Haverford and immediately loved the all-boys environment. Every single teacher seemed to offer incredible amounts of support to each student. My family and I decided that I would go, right then and there. I was elated to find out that Wills would also be joining me at Haverford, as he was having some challenges at Episcopal. My parents hoped that the move would help us with school work and maturity. My brother was not excited to transfer schools, but I was happy that we would be starting a new journey together. As the school year ended, I said goodbye to my core group of friends and all of my classmates at Episcopal. I was upset that I would no longer be able to see my best friends every day and realized that I was going to have to make all new friends at a brand new school. It was an unbelievably difficult decision.

Even though I regret leaving my old friends at Episcopal, I have come to realize that transferring to Haverford was one of the best decisions that my parents and I have ever made. I was immature for an eighth-grader. I was struggling to understand and accept my disability — I just wasn't ready to move up to ninth grade at the time. That summer, I used my free time to reach out to new classmates and prepare myself for a new school. It was the beginning of a new chapter, and I couldn't wait to get started.

Year Fifteen

I started my first day at the Haverford School on September 8, 2013. Surprisingly, I was accepted as part of the brotherhood right way. My classmates reached out to me to see if I needed anything and began asking me to hang out after school. Immediately, I felt right at home. Transferring into a new school can be difficult, and I am so glad that I had my friends as well as my family to lean on. They made my transition so much easier.

Haverford is an all-boys school, so not having any girls in my classes was an adjustment. After a couple of days, I began to realize the benefit of not having girls as a distraction. I paid attention in class for longer periods of time and was able to schedule meetings with my teachers whenever I wanted. Looking back, the all-boys environment made me feel more at home and also allowed me to become closer with my new friends more quickly than usual. I found out that the schoolwork was not going to be as hard as it had been at Episcopal, but that was probably only because I was retaking the same classes.

Nevertheless, I regained confidence in my intelligence and in my work ethic. I got my grades back up and decided to try out for the football team at the start of the fall. One day after tryouts, I came home to discover that the growth hormones were finally starting to work. My mother checked my height and was excited to tell me that I had grown 3 inches over the summer. A smile immediately washed over my face. I was getting bigger and could finally start to build muscle on my right side. In the meantime, my new orthotics helped with my limp, and I was able to find better ways to hide my disability while on the field.

We finished tryouts, and I played well enough to earn a starting spot at either cornerback or safety. I did not want to play offense because I was too scared that my disability would be exposed; I still was not able to carry the ball with my right hand. I ended up playing most of the season at cornerback and honestly, I loved it. I especially loved the camaraderie that my teammates and I shared. They did not care that I used to go to Episcopal, our arch-rival, or that I still had friends there. None of the teams in our league ever ran pass plays, so I learned how to leave my position early and converge on the running back. I always hit with my left shoulder and actually made 4 or 5 tackles for my team that year.

In my first season playing squash for the Fords, I was introduced to the team and quickly discovered that tryouts for Haverford were going to be much different than Episcopal's had been. I played four matches against my new teammates and unfortunately lost all of them. I thought that I was in good shape and I thought that I would be competitive, but I was wrong. I lost every match in three games, and my new coach was forced to put me in the number five position to start the season. It was two spots lower than I had played on Episcopal's team, but I did not care. There was nothing that I could do about it. Haverford's squash team was better and the competition was much more intense.

Around this time in the season, my mood improved and I became a happier person all around. I had adjusted to my new school and was doing reasonably well in the classroom. I continued to train at Scozzie and prepare myself for the season. Even though I was playing number five on the team, I was excited. I was training with other great junior players, day in and day out. It was a fantastic time for me to get better and simply work on my game. I was nervous when the season finally started, but ended up winning every match except for two. I lost both of my matches in the semi-finals and finals of the Inter-Ac tournament. We finished the year and went into US Squash Middle School team championships as the #2 seed. The experience was unlike anything I had ever been a part of. The atmosphere at Yale University, and especially in the Brady Squash Center, was electric!

Fortunately, my teammates and I cruised through the first three rounds and found ourselves in the championship against Greenwich Country Day School. Right before we were scheduled to go on, my coach told me that I would be playing first on the show court. I was so nervous that I sweat through my shirt before even walking on court. I was scared; I did not want any of the spectators to see, or comment on, my limp. I spent the entire warm-up stretching out my ankle; I think that it was one of the most nerve-racking experiences of my life. I looked up and saw about 30 spectators watching me from the crowd. Playing on a squash court is like being on display in a fishbowl. There was truly nowhere for me to hide. I strolled onto the show court and started hitting forehand rails to warm up. My opponent walked on court and looked as cool and calm as ever. He was only a seventh-grader, and though I was ranked and rated higher than him, I was nervous. I should have won the match easily, but I did not.

Much to my surprise, he started taking the ball short within five shots every rally. He was trying to bait me to commit unforced errors, and honestly, it worked. I made mistake after mistake; I was pissed at myself. I came off the court dripping in sweat. As I looked at the lineups, I realized that Greenwich Country Day School matched up with our team pretty evenly. If I did not win my individual match, my teammates and I had a real chance to lose the match overall. In order to win, I had to tune out my stroke, tune out all of the spectators, and just play squash. So that is precisely what I did. I took the match 3-1, and my victory meant that my teammates and I were one step closer to winning the Middle School National Championship. Two wins later, we secured the victory. We brought the banner back to the Haverford School and celebrated. I was happy and proud of myself.

I spent the rest of the winter training at Scozzie. I hung out with my new classmates and started playing Lacrosse again. As the spring season began, I picked up my Lacrosse stick and tried to find time to hit the wall every day. At the time, winning championships in squash felt great, but I remained steadfast in my pursuit of reaching Division I Lacrosse. I still wanted to be just like my father.

By this time, I was able to get over my disappointment about missing the cut for Fever and ended up deciding to try out for the team again. I was now part of the 2018 graduation year, and I thought that making the team would be easy, but I was wrong. I still couldn't carry the ball effectively with my right hand and, as a result, most of my defenders started to take advantage of me. By the end of the scrimmage, I had been stripped of the ball twice; I could not even put a point in the board. I felt awful. I had played terribly.

Unfortunately, I did not perform much better in school tryouts. The Haverford School team was much more competitive than Episcopal's team. I was blown away by the talent of my peers. Since Haverford is an all-boys school, it meant that we had twice as many boys tryout for the Lacrosse team than they did. As I finished tryouts, I was not aware that I had only made the team because I was an eighth-grader. At first, I was excited, but came to the realization that I was

The First Twenty

going to spend most of the season riding the bench. I rarely saw the field and scored my only goal of the year during a blowout loss to a non-league team. My limp was more noticeable and because I could not carry the ball to my right hand, I became a "sitting duck" of sorts. *If I was not even good enough to start for my eighth-grade team, how would I ever play for a college program?* I slowly started to see my dream fade away.

BOOK V

THE HIGH SCHOOL YEARS

(9/17/2014)

Year Sixteen

I started my first day of ninth-grade on September 6, 2014. Almost immediately, I realized that high school would prove to be a considerable change in my life. I reached back out to my old Episcopal friends for help. They told me that high school would be much more difficult, and yet much more enjoyable. I found myself spending a lot of time in the library. I was not used to having so much freedom in between classes. M y schedule was tailored specifically for me and, sadly, my friends were not in any of my classes. It took a while for me to get used to only seeing them at lunch or during my free periods. At the beginning of the semester, I struggled with finding my classes and turning my homework in on time, but eventually I got the hang of it.

In the fall, it was apparent that I needed to move on from football. I was small and weak. I could not imagine going against twelfth-graders. After discussing it with my parents, I decided to try out for the golf team instead. My parents both play golf, so they taught me how to swing and told me the basic rules of the game. I practiced a fair amount leading up to the tryouts and played well enough to make the Junior Varsity team.

Unfortunately, we were only allowed access to the course twice a week, so I spent my off days and weekends training at Scozzie. And though I liked playing golf and being out on the course, I was nowhere near good enough to play in matches. Golf had always been a sport that I had taken less seriously, so I was not disappointed. I was distracted with squash and decided to spend all of my free time preparing for the upcoming winter season. I found myself playing in back to back US Squash tournaments as the fall season came to a close.

The first was a Gold at the University of Virginia and the second was a local Silver. We arrived at the MacArthur Squash Center on a rainy Friday at 2 PM, and I prepared to play my first match of the weekend. I was surprised to find the atmosphere to be very similar to that of the US Squash Team Championships. As I warmed up for my first match, I told my father that the competition might be a bit out of my league. When my opponent walked on court, he did not even look at me; he simply went over to the right wall and started warming up his

The First Twenty

backhand. We spun a racket to decide who would serve, and after the break, my opponent came out on fire. We finished the match just as quickly as we had started it. I could not believe that I had lost without a fight. The match was over just like that; he blew me out in a comfortable three games. I was so disappointed that I hung my head for the rest of the day.

    I was knocked out of the tournament two matches later with a loss in the consolation semi-finals, and made my father drove me home immediately after the match. I did not want to stick around and watch any of my friends win while I was merely a spectator. On the ride back home, my father and I discussed my freshman year at school. I was doing pretty well in the classroom and having moderate success in squash, but Lacrosse was a whole different story. My father was honest with me and told me that I would, most likely, not play on the Varsity Lacrosse team until my senior year because of how good my competition was going to be. The Haverford School's Lacrosse program has been a perennial powerhouse for years, and because of my disability, I would not be able to earn much playing time. My father comforted me as best he could, but I would not open up to him. *If only I had been born normal, none of this would've happened.* I whispered to myself as I choked back tears.

    Ever since I could walk, my dream had always been to be a Division I Lacrosse player - just like my father. I had to stand by and watch helplessly over the years as my friends improved, while I felt like I was stuck in quicksand. It was awful. I curled up in a ball and was silent for the rest of the ride home. I felt like I had let my father down, but I was wrong. He pulled the car into our garage and immediately hugged me. He said softly, "Tyler, you've overcome so much. You are amazing. I am so proud." At that moment, I lost it. I began to realize that I had always been too deep in my own head and that my father had been right all along. We sat in the back of his car and cried together. I hugged him as I told him that I was done with Lacrosse; I was not having fun playing the sport anymore. I did not want to sit the bench for four more years. When I got out of the car, I understood that my father loved me for who I was. And the moment we had just shared together was one of the happiest moments of my life.

    As I played my second squash tournament of the fall, I realized how badly I did not want a repeat of my performances from previous

Silver tournaments. I cruised through the first two rounds and won my semi-final match in a five-game thriller. I still do not understand how I won that match. I was not playing as well as I should have, and I made so many unforced errors. Somehow, I came back to win the fifth game and moved on to the finals. In the finals, I was matched up against Ryan York, a freshman from St. Paul's in Baltimore, Maryland. He was a grinder and relentlessly worked to retrieve every ball. Our match was long and grueling. As I prepared to serve for match point, I looked to my parents and coaches in the crowd. I was distracted, but luckily, my opponent hit his return of serve into the tin. I pumped my fists in excitement. I had done it! I had just won my first ever US Squash tournament. I exited the court and ran to hug my parents. Even though it was only a Silver, I finally had a "W" under my belt and it felt terrific!

I rode the "high" of my tournament win into school tryouts. I discovered that since the Haverford School has a talented squash program, our coaches decided to form two Varsity teams, Varsity "A" and Varsity "B". Varsity "A" would only play the top competition in high school; while Varsity "B" would play most of the squash programs "....in the surrounding area and also compete in a lower division of High School Nationals. I was overconfident and unfortunately started the tryouts by dropping three of my opening four matches. I was placed on the Varsity "B" team at the number #6 position. And though I was disappointed in my performance, there was nothing I could do. That is one of the great things about individual sports — it's all up to you.

I played the season out and had a pretty successful year. I ended with a record of five wins and only two losses. At the end of the season, our coach informed us that my teammates and I had played well enough to qualify for the B division of High School Nationals. We traveled to Avon Old Farms for the tournament, and thankfully, my matches were not competitive in the #6 position. I won every single one of them in three games, but unfortunately, my teammates did not have the same amount of success. We ended up losing in the semi-finals to one of our rivals, The Shipley School, and my teammates and I were pissed about it.

As the winter turned to spring, I decided to try out for the tennis team. It was my first spring season since about second grade where I did not touch a Lacrosse stick. From the tennis courts, I watched as most of my friends walked across the turf to get to Lacrosse practice. I

The First Twenty

longed to be out there and among them. I missed the sport and being part of a team more than anything. I tried my best to block it out of my head - Lacrosse was just not an option for me anymore. The only reason that I was still playing squash was because it was a great workout and because it helped strengthen my left side. I never thought that I would be able to play in college. For a while, I continued to play sports only because it was a school requirement.

I started the tennis season and thought that I was going to have moderate success in match-play because of my squash game, but I was wrong. I brought my ankle brace over from squash, and even though it helped to stabilize my ankle, the movement patterns in the two sports are completely different. On the tennis court, my limp was much more noticeable, and my teammates started asking if I was okay. They could tell that something was wrong. They suggested that I go see the trainer or sit out of practice, but I lied and told them that I was healthy. I brushed off their questions and explained to my coaches that I was recovering from a broken ankle. I did not know if they believed me, but I did not care. I would do anything to keep my stroke a secret. I was too afraid to be judged and rejected by others. I did not want them to make fun of my disability. I was not yet mature enough to be okay with just being myself.

I ended up making the JV tennis team in the fourth-doubles position, but unfortunately, my partner and I were not good enough to play in any matches or to even travel with the team. I was able to practice with the team, and as the season went on, my teammates started to ask about my ankle more and more. During pickup basketball one day, some of my classmates noticed that I could not move the individual fingers on my right hand and started to make fun of me for it. That, in combination with my teammates telling the rest of the school about the extent of my limp, turned their harmless jokes into bullying. It was a nightmare, and all I could do was sit back and take it. I decided not to tell my parents because I thought that it would only make the teasing worse. I did not know what to do, so I tried my best to act like the comments just did not exist. I had a pretty good group of friends with whom I texted almost every night and hung out with on weekends, but things seemed to change when the teasing escalated. I noticed that they were not inviting me to hang out as often and sometimes "forgot" to answer my texts. At the time, I did not blame them. I was different, and in high school, people shy away from different.

I went about my daily routine and pretended not to notice as some of my classmates made fun of me. They would mock the way that my right hand looked and often snapchat it to their friends. One time, I even saw one of my classmates walking around the library with a limp, calling it the "Burt Walk," and laughing. He did not know that I had seen him, but he and some of his friends were mocking me to almost every other student in my grade. They got a laugh from nearly everybody. I have a pretty thick skin, so the comments did not get to me, but I could not stand to see them mock me. It was humiliating. I could sometimes hear my classmates whisper to each other and laugh as I walked into the library or changed classes. The teasing broke down my self-confidence; it was a demoralizing.

One day in late April, I hit my breaking point and asked my parents to transfer schools. I just wanted to get away. I want to distance myself from my disability and never bring it up again. I fell back into the deep and dark corners of my thoughts. I struggled to find the motivation to get out of bed every morning. I spent hours every night curled up in my room and would cry my eyes out. Thankfully, I was able to finish out the school year with my family's support. It was tough—the hurtful comments kept coming and showed no signs of stopping.

In response, I grabbed a rubber band and started to put it on my right wrist every day before school. I promised myself that I would never respond to the kids who bullied me, but that I would at least snap my wrist with the rubber band every time I heard a mean comment or after realizing that someone was making fun of me. I continued with my normal routine, and after a while, the pain felt almost normal. I did not know it at the time, but I was subconsciously proving to myself that their words could not hurt me. That I was stronger than anything they could throw my way.

On the second to the last day of exams, one of my classmates verbally committed to play Division I Lacrosse. I watched as everyone celebrated and congratulated him in the library. One of the kids who repeatedly teased me immediately went up to him and offered his congratulations. "Congratulations, man, congrats! D1, that's unbelievable. I wish I could be a D1 athlete. You must be so excited,

The First Twenty

that's crazy!" I walked away as soon as he finished his sentence. It was unbelievable. I saw firsthand how much they celebrated my classmate just because he was going to become a Division 1 athlete.

When I got home, I took out my computer. I googled: "stroke survivors who became Division I athletes," and the search results came up empty. I knew that I was not going to be a Division I Lacrosse player, but that did not mean that I could not become a Division I athlete. In squash, there is only is only Division 1, so it was by far, the best chance I had to succeed. Before I went to bed that night, I made myself a promise. I was feeling lonelier and more vulnerable than ever. I decided, right then and there, that squash was going to be my way out. I stared at the ceiling, asking God for his help and guidance. I closed my eyes and told myself that there was a chance that I could become the first-ever stroke survivor to compete in men's Division I athletics. I said it out loud, over and over again. I did not care that it had never been done before; I was ready to write my own history. I wanted to prove everyone wrong. Suddenly, I realized that my lifelong dream had changed. I understood that I was not meant to follow my father's path—I was meant to pave my own way. And squash was going to be the way that I would do it. Once I became a Division I athlete, I knew that my classmates would see me in a different light. I would prove to them, and myself, that I could do anything despite my deficit.

I spent my summer becoming obsessed with turning my dream into reality. I choose not to play in any squash tournaments and instead underwent extensive physical therapy for my right angle. Every day, I continued to push and tried to improve my game. I started to fall in love with the grind both on and off the court. I never quit or backed out of a challenge and told myself that I was just as good as any 'normal' person. I started training at Scozzie five times a week and gradually saw my numbers on the Versaclimber, the stationary bike, and the Batak rise.

Just as school was about to start, I passed my learners permit test at the DMV and began learning how to drive a car. It was stressful, but I enjoyed the freedom that came with age. I was getting older and becoming more mature. I could not wait to end the summer and start my tenth-grade year.

Year Seventeen

I started my first day of tenth grade on September 6, 2015. By this time, I had grown accustomed to the workload of a high school student and began to feel comfortable in the classroom. This was the year I realized that I had very few close friends. Even though most of my classmates would still say "hi" to me in the hallways and sit with me at lunch, I knew that they would secretly make fun of me behind my back. Sometimes I felt like I was on an island, and all alone. Although I have always had my family to talk to, I did not have that core group of friends. It was upsetting. There were days when I felt like my relationships with my classmates were just for show.

I used the rubber band occasionally throughout my tenth-grade year and learned just to let the comments roll off my back. I began to adopt the motto "treat others the way you want to be treated" because I understood how much damage bullying can do to a person, and I would not wish it on my worst enemy. I tried out for the golf team again in the fall and barely made the Junior Varsity team. I began the year by practicing with the team and actually played in the final match of the season because of an injury to one of my teammates.

I spent a majority of my free time either going to Scozzie or studying in the library, and tried to keep my grades up. I knew that if I was going to get recruited, then I would have to meet the necessary grade point average requirements and earn a respectable standardized test score. It was time for me to buckle down. I began taking school work more seriously and saw it as a necessary step on the road to achieving my dream. It was tough for me to stay focused, but I forced myself to grind it out. I locked myself in my room for hours every night and had tutors over on the weekend. It was more challenging than I could ever imagine.

Before I knew it, squash tryouts were right at my doorstep. I hoped that this would be the first year I made the jump to the Varsity "A" team. I passed my license test two days before tryouts and started driving myself and my brother to school every day. My freedom was short-lived though because I spun out and crashed my car into a telephone pole within a week. I broke my nose on the steering wheel. I

The First Twenty

still can't figure out why the airbags never deployed. It was one of the scariest moments of my life.

Nevertheless, I took the weekend off and was back for the start of match play on Monday afternoon. And though the bleeding had stopped, it took a while for me to get used to breathing out of only one nostril. I felt different, and it was painful. Unfortunately, I had little success in tryouts. I moved up two positions on the ladder because we graduated two seniors from the previous year's team, but that was about it. I lost two of my opening three matches during tryouts and was left off of Varsity "A" for the second year in a row. When our coach announced the roster, I was so disappointed that I immediately sprinted to my car. Tears started streaming down my face, and I screamed at myself for not putting enough work in. I forced myself to drive to Scozzie and I soloed for hours. From then on, I told myself that my losses were going to motivate me to play better and to train even harder.

Two weeks later, I began to gather the necessary materials for the SAT and started meeting with a tutor who specialized in standardized testing. I took some preliminary quizzes and found out pretty quickly that the SAT was going to be unbelievably difficult for me. I ran out of time on every section and often left most of the bubbles partially filled in or sometimes even completely blank. My tutor tried his best to encourage me. "Grind it out. I promise you that you will get better eventually. Just put in the work. "You got this." I trusted him, but quickly found myself buried under a mountain of work as I started league play for the Varsity "B" team. Surprisingly, I actually won some matches against opponents who were rated and ranked higher than me to start the year. In those matches, I either played really well or really poorly. There was no in-between. Some days I would win against an opponent rated much higher than me, and other days I would choke against players who I had beaten easily the year before. Thankfully, I ended the season with a winning record and was lucky enough to have my teammates carry me to the US Squash High School team championships.

Our team qualified for the "B" division of High School Nationals and played pretty well throughout the entire tournament. I went 4 - 1, but my teammates and I lost a heartbreaking match to the Groton School in the semi-finals. We did not focus on our match for long though, because we went to the other venue to watch the Varsity "A" play in the National Championship against Brunswick. Brunswick is one of Haverford's oldest rivals in squash and Lacrosse. This match was my first taste of the rivalry, and there was not an open seat in the house. You could not even tie your shoe without bumping into people. I wanted nothing more than to win such a crucial match on that kind of stage. I sat down next to the rest of my teammates and eagerly cheered on my squad. Unfortunately, Brunswick's lineup was too talented, and they ended up stealing the championship from us. I could see the disappointment hang on my teammates' faces. It was not the way both of our teams wanted to end the season.

I had seen what it was like to play in the biggest high school match of the year, and I promised myself that I would be there one day. As I settled back in at home, I put my squash racket back in its bag and tried to swim through a mountain of SAT practice tests. I was not able to complete a full test before I had to call my tutor and tell him that there was a problem. The practice tests were too complicated, and I had trouble raising my score because I made careless errors in every section. My tutor came back over to the house, and we quickly realized that I was running out of time on every attempt. I still do not know why I am wired this way, but I always get incredibly nervous in timed situations. I had flashbacks of Mr. Hark's minute clinic. It was disheartening. I was never able to score what I needed to get recruited.

After more failed attempts, my tutor suggested that I switch the ACT. He came back a week later and administered two practice - ACT's over a period of three weeks. I did not do well, but he forced me to stick with the ACT and gave me more practice tests. Even though I was disappointed, I was glad that I did not have to take the SAT. The math sections were too difficult, and they made my head spin. *At least the ACT is a little bit more my speed;* I thought to myself as I took the stack of books back to my room. *Back to the grind.*

I tried out for the tennis team for the third year in a row and, not surprisingly, made the Junior Varsity team once again. Early on, I decided that I would not take the season too seriously because I wanted to use all of my time to focus on getting better at squash. Even though tennis is a great way to stay in shape and enjoy the weather, it was not like I was going to kill myself over the sport. I had already fully committed to becoming a collegiate squash player. I still received some

The First Twenty

questions about my limp, and I knew that teammates made fun of me behind my back, but I just brushed it off. They had no idea what was coming; they had no idea who I was going to become. I continued to use my rubber band every day, and eventually, their teasing just became a part of my normal routine.

Summer approached rapidly, and though I had planned to use my time to study for the ACT and to train for squash, my parents did not see it that way. My father told me it was time for me to get a job. I put in applications at a bunch of restaurants in the area and only received a few responses. On the application forms, I purposely left out the fact that I suffered a stroke because I was embarrassed about it and also because I thought that I could do anything that a "normal" person could do. To this day, I have never told myself that I am too weak or too disabled for anything. One of the only restaurants to respond to my job application was 333 Belrose Bar and Grill, and thankfully, their manager decided to hire me as a busboy for the summer.

Belrose is located only fifteen minutes from my house, and I could not wait to start working. I could not wait to make my own money. After completing three training shifts, I was added to the final schedule for the summer and was ready to go. I started working three to four nights a week from 3:30 PM to 10 PM. The work was exhausting, and I was treated like dirt, but it was the greatest job that I have ever had. It truly taught me the value of a dollar and also taught me fundamental lessons about how to be a man. I had to learn how to take responsibility for my actions and looking back, cannot thank my father enough for forcing me to get that first job. I learned different ways to compensate for my disability while carrying the bins of dirty dishes, pouring water, or putting out the place settings. It was not easy, but I persevered. Working for Belrose was one of the best decisions that I have ever made.

Year Eighteen

I started my first day of eleventh grade on September 14, 2016. I had finally become an upperclassman and started to enjoy the freedom that came with junior year. I got to pick most of my classes and could also schedule my own free periods. In September, I attended my first ever peer counseling session. Peer counseling was a student-led group that met twice a month during our lunch block. In the meetings, we discussed various issues within our community — from life stories to daily struggles. I loved peer counseling because no topic was ever really off-limits. Different seniors were featured in front of the group weekly, and each of them had a different story to tell. I am not ashamed to admit that I broke down in tears multiple times while listening to them. Yes, I was born with a life-altering disability, but I struggled to believe some of the obstacles my classmates were also trying to overcome. I heard first-hand stories of domestic abuse and drug addiction in the inner-city. I heard stories that were so far out of my realm of understanding that I almost did not believe them.

As the stories resonated with me, I finally began to realize that I was not fighting alone. My mother has always said that "everyone is fighting their own battles" and that "everyone is going through something, whether you see it or not does not actually matter." I never believed her until that moment. She was right all along. I used to think that my disability was the single worst thing in the world, and peer counseling changed my mind. I started learning how to voice my appreciation for my family as well as for my friends. They made me into the person that I am today; I will always be grateful. As I continued the school year, I began attending peer counseling sessions regularly. I tried out for the golf team in the fall but did not shoot as well as I thought I could have. I ended up making the Junior Varsity team for the third year in a row. It was not disheartening, though, because I thought to myself: *the more free time, the better.*

In the fall, I was able to earn the necessary grades to open my recruitment and started to email prospective coaches at universities around the country. I wanted to gauge their interest. I included a squash resume and detailed the tournaments that I had played in as

The First Twenty

well as the relevant matches that I had won. At the time, I was ranked 87th in the country for BU19 and had a rating of 4.92.

Obviously, my resume was not impressive enough to grab the attention of the top squash schools, but it was definitely good enough to get recruited. I knew that I was ranked and rated high enough to play college squash; I just had to find a coach to take a chance on me. I emailed the coaches from Dickinson, Hobart, Haverford, and the entirety of the New England Small College Athletic Conference (NESCAC).

A couple of weeks passed, and I took my first real ACT. It was stressful. I found the ACT to be vastly different from all of my practice packets. I was unable to finish the math or science section in time. Immediately upon leaving the testing center, I knew that I would have to retake my ACT at least two more times in order to feel confident about my score. I called my parents on the drive home and told them how upset I was. Surprisingly, they were unbelievably supportive. "Keep grinding," they told me. "You can give it another go! You are good. You got this." Their words made me feel so much better.

Suddenly, it was time to start squash season again. Three seniors had graduated from the previous year's team, and I went into tryouts excited for the opportunity to crack the Varsity "A" roster. I played two matches in our opening round-robin and won both of them. I was finally able to see the light at the end of the tunnel. By the end of the tryouts, I was ranked number 10 on the ladder. I was overjoyed. I was only one spot away from starting on Varsity "A." I ended the week by challenging up to the #9 spot on the roster and won the match by the skin of my teeth. My opponent knew my game inside and out because we trained together every day, so I decided to slow the pace down and completely switch up my game plan. I was able to squeeze out the victory, 3 - 1, and I could not have been happier. I walked off court and high-fived my teammates and coaches. *I was finally a member of Varsity "A."* My dream was slowly starting to come to fruition.

Around this time, the social media app Instagram had become more relevant because of a new feature that allowed its users to share videos with their followers. I had never been self-conscious about Instagram and social media in general until they introduced this feature. It was difficult to share videos of myself because I was not yet ready to show the world that I was disabled. I did not want everyone on the internet to make fun of me. As my friends and classmates integrated this new feature into their daily lives, I started to fade Instagram out of my life. I was too scared that my followers would judge me. I just wanted to be seen as another normal guy. Later that day, I got my ACT results back by email and was not too pleased with the results. I did not get my desired score and was pretty dismayed; I had to push myself to work even harder. I decided to double down and did not pick my head up from my ACT booklet for the next month. I needed a good score so that I could make my dream come true. I retook the ACT a month later and left the testing center feeling relieved and excited. Even though the math and science sections were the toughest, I was able to balance out my poor performance by doing well on the reading section. I was overjoyed.

I rode my newfound confidence into the squash season and even surprised myself with how well I performed. I had grown accustomed to playing (and losing) against the top three players from other varsity schools, so I easily defeated my opponents in the #9 position. As we moved into High School Nationals, I received my second ACT score back and screamed in excitement upon learning that I had earned a score high enough to get me a recruitment spot at most of the schools around the country. I realized that I was one step closer to achieving my dream. Later that week, I received follow-up emails and interest from Dickinson, Colby, Amherst, Bowdoin, Wesleyan, and Hobart.

As our team arrived at Nationals, I proceeded to set up visits to those colleges for the spring. Unfortunately, I had to play on the Varsity "B" team because US Squash only allows each team to field seven players for High School Nationals. It ended up being a blessing in disguise. My teammates and I cruised through the first two rounds and found ourselves competing against one of our league rivals, the Shipley School, in the semi-finals. The match ended up being one of the most important of my entire career. We lost the opening three matches to Shipley and were down 3 - 2 with only our number one, P.J. Rodden, and myself left to play. We warmed up together and prepared to walk on court with everything on the line. We were only one loss away from elimination. I was not playing in a National Championship, but the pressure was all on my shoulders. It felt like 50 spectators were split between the two courts. My opponent, Fitz Simmons, was a senior and

The First Twenty

had committed to Haverford college earlier in the school year. He was projected to play #1 for them as an incoming freshman, and I almost hyperventilated when my father told me that I would be playing him. I tried to distract myself and went on the court to warm up. I took a deep breath; it was finally my time.

We started the match, and I took a defensive position right from the start. My opponent cut every ball off before the back wall, and I struggled to keep up. I was losing every point and became angry at myself. I let him string together eight points in a row, and he ended up taking the first game, 11 - 6. I left the court, went straight through the front doors, and sat down on a bench outside the building. I could not get my hands to stop shaking. I tried to calm myself down. As I re-entered the Athletic Center, I heard the roar from P.J.'s court. He had just won his match. We were all tied up at 3 - 3; it was down to me. I tried my best to forget about the last game and clear my head, but it was difficult. We started the second game, and Fitz retook the offensive position right from the start. He ran me from corner to corner and easily won the first three points of the game. *No... No... No...* I thought. *This cannot be happening.* On the next point, he served an easy lob; I drilled it right into the tin. I had lost my head. He won the game 11 - 7 and stormed off court. He was hype. It was time to regroup.

As I walked into the hallway, I hung my head. I was down 2 - 0 and only one more game away from elimination. My teammates tried to cheer me up, but their facial expressions told a completely different story. They did not come outside to coach me and instead started to pack up their bags. They thought that we were going home. I sat on the outdoor bench with my head in my hands. I was speechless. I could not believe that I was going to let my team down. I was almost entirely out of options—all I could do was pull off a miracle. My father left the crowd and came outside to console me. He came over and hugged me. "Tyler," he told me, "I know how you are going to win. Listen." He pulled me close. "Volley everything. Do not care about losing or anything — Volley everything. You are going to lose anyway, so volley everything. Why not try? Trust me."

I started the third game with a pit in my stomach. All of the pressure was on me. Much to my dismay, Fitz came out on fire and won the first three points of the game. I could hear my father urging me on in the back of my head. I stuck with the game plan and rattled off nine points in a row. I fist-pumped to the crowd and started to feel the momentum shift in the match. I won the third game 11 - 7 and immediately ran off court. I could not contain my excitement. I paced back and forth outside of the Athletic Center and choked down a bottle of water. My father was right.

I went on to win the next two games and take the match 3 - 2. I could not believe it. My teammates waited for me to shake hands and then rushed the court to mob me. As we celebrated and they chanted my name, I raised my arms in triumph. I had done it! Despite my stroke and all of my setbacks, I felt like a champion. I won the match for my school and my teammates. There was no better feeling in the world. I exited the court and immediately found my parents. I wrapped them in a sweaty hug and could not stop celebrating. I made sure to thank my father. It was one of the happiest moments of my life. We won the match 4 - 3 and moved onto the next round.

Unfortunately, our luck quickly ran out. We were overconfident going into our final match and lost to the McDonogh School in a blowout. My captains and I were so upset that we hardly said a word to each other for the entire bus ride back to campus. And even though my teammates and I did not end the season the way that we wanted to, my match against the Shipley School was something that I will never forget.

Throughout the spring, I visited Dickinson, Wesleyan, Colby, Amherst, Bowdoin, and Haverford College. And although I was not initially offered a recruitment spot, most of my visits went well. I loved every single college that I traveled to and longed for the chance to be a member of their squash programs. In the middle of April, the Colby College men's head coach, Sakhi Khan, called and asked me to come up to Colby for a follow-up visit. I spent the day with his team, and they took me to the courts early one Saturday morning. Initially, Coach Khan was skeptical about my ankle and my movement patterns. He questioned whether or not I would have the stamina to play collegiate squash. But as the weekend continued, I was able to convince him that I would be a welcome addition to his team because I beat one of his top-ranked players. He was impressed and decided to recruit me. Hours later, Coach Khan called me into his office and offered me a recruitment spot during an hour-long meeting. It was a day I will never

The First Twenty

forget, April 16, 2017. I committed on the spot. I left his office that day in tears — I was one step closer to achieving my dream.

I returned home and celebrated the news with my family. It was the happiest I had ever been; it almost felt surreal. I was a stroke survivor, and yet I was going to become a Division I athlete. Just saying it out loud sounded crazy. I noticed a change of attitude from my teammates and classmates as they found out about my commitment. Almost immediately, they stopped making fun of me. They stopped talking behind my back and started congratulating me to my face. I was moved to tears a couple of times as I reminisced on how far I had come.

Since the pressure had been taken off of my shoulders, I spent the summer relaxing and rejuvenating. I picked up dinner shifts at Belrose and spent most of my free time at Scozzie. I worked day in and day out to improve my game, and I could not wait to play at the next level. In August, I was contacted by Ms. Heed, a faculty leader of peer counseling, and asked if I would be one of the senior leaders of the group for the upcoming year. Ms. Heed is a terrific lady who knew the extent of my disability better than most of the teachers at Haverford. She thought that I was an inspiration and wanted me to share my story with the group. I immediately agreed and went into my final year of high school with a brand new attitude.

Year Nineteen

I started my first day of twelfth grade on September 6, 2017. I had picked my courses for the year over the summer and was excited to take new and exciting classes like Social Psychology and United States Government. Senior year was the first year where I truly started to be myself. I cared less about what my friends were into and started exploring my own interests. I promised myself that I was no longer going to be a follower. I began the year by organizing peer counseling sessions and became comfortable telling my story to a crowd of people. Getting my secret off of my chest was more liberating than I could ever imagine. I was excited to show the world who I really was.

I tried out for the golf team in the fall and made Junior Varsity for the fourth year in a row. Younger players came onto the scene and pushed me off of the Varsity roster. I have always been competitive and wanted to keep up with them, but I was just not good enough. I never took golf too seriously though, and just enjoyed playing for fun. I figured that I would use my free time to focus on squash. At this point in my life, I was in a very good space mentally. I could not believe how far I had come. Just four years earlier, I struggled to find the motivation to get out of bed in the morning. I hated my life because of my disability and grappled with bouts of depression. And now, I was completely different. I felt like I had a million reasons to get up in the morning and a million more reasons to keep going. I began to set small goals for myself every morning before getting dressed for school. I was more motivated than ever before.

I trained for squash almost every day and reclaimed the number nine position on the ladder at the start of tryouts. That season, I played everywhere from #9 to #4 because of injuries to my teammates. I won most of my matches and used my losses as motivation and preparation for the collegiate level. I applied to college and was accepted to Colby as a member of the class of 2022. I watched my friends and classmates struggle with the anxiety of the college process and was extremely thankful for my commitment. We finished out the season, and I found myself stuck at the #8 position on the ladder. I was a substitute for Varsity "A" in my last ever High School Nationals, and honestly, it was upsetting. I wanted to be out there. I wanted to go to battle with my teammates, but sometimes life does not go the way that you pictured it going.

I watched and cheered from the sidelines as my team battled their way through the tournament and eventually found themselves in the final and competing for a National Championship. At the match, the atmosphere was unbelievable. Unfortunately, the Brunswick team caught fire and won four matches in a row to take the national championship from us, 5 - 2. I looked around and felt bad for all of my guys. They left everything on the court and still came up short. It was a heartbreaking loss and an even more painful bus ride home.

When the spring came around, I did not try out for the tennis team because seniors are only required to play two sports. I used the much-needed free time to get back on the squash court and continue my training. I got myself into great shape, and everything seemed going well until my right ankle started to supinate more than usual. When my mother decided to set up an appointment with our orthopedic doctor, I was scared to attend the meeting because I knew that she was going to recommend an Achilles lengthening surgery. It was not necessary at this particular moment in time, but the procedure should be done by 2022. We met with DuPont's orthopedic surgeon, Dr. Louise Reid Nichols, and discussed options. After mulling it over with my parents, I decided not to go through with the surgery. There were just too many question marks. I did not know if I would ever be the same player after my surgery and was not willing to miss the chance at achieving my dream. My mother strongly urged me to reconsider my decision. She desperately wanted me to get the surgery, but there were just too many question marks. I told myself that I could survive one more year without it.

I graduated high school on June 8, 2018. It was a bittersweet ending to my five years at the Haverford School. I made some of my best and closest friends at Haverford. And although my circle was small, I was extremely tight with my friends. I knew that I might not see some of my best friends for months, or maybe even years. I still am nostalgic about it to this day; I miss those guys. That summer, I decided not to return to Belrose and instead got a job valeting cars for different restaurants in the Delaware County area. The hours were long, and the shifts were uninteresting. It was hard for me to concentrate. I was always bored out of my mind. I worked three to four nights a week, from four in the afternoon until ten at night. As I became comfortable with the hours, I started to spend every morning and most of my off days training at Scozzie. Even though it was not the most fun or exciting way to spend my senior summer, I did not care. I realized how close I was to achieving my dream and promised myself that I was going to work as hard as possible to make it a reality. The hours were long and the shifts were uninteresting.

    Summer came to a close, and I reluctantly started packing for college. It was tough to say goodbye to my family; I had never really been away from them for an extended period of time I was upset for a while about it, but soon realized that it marked the start of a new chapter in my life. Whether I liked it or not, my world was changing. I had to come to terms with it. I was sad, but this was the year that I would accomplish my dream. I was ready for it. I slowly moved my belongings to the downstairs hallway and said goodbye to all of my friends. I was the only student from my graduating class set to attend Colby and I began to feel lonely as my friends left, one by one.

    I was going to have to make new friends in a brand new environment. It felt like my move to Haverford all over again. Only this time, I was not sure if I would be happy. I was going to have a new roommate whom I had never met before. It was scary. I began to ask myself how my new friends and classmates would react to my disability. *Would they see me as just another one of them? Were they going to distance themselves from me simply because I was different?* A million questions popped into my head as I prepared to make the nine and a half-hour drive up to Waterville, Maine.

BOOK VI

THE COLLEGE YEAR &

MORE

(8/26/2018)

Year Twenty

On August 26, I packed up my final belongings and said goodbye to my family. I got a little bit choked up as I got in the car and gave my brother one last hug. I was grateful that both of my parents agreed to make the 9 ½ hour drive to drop me off at Colby. We talked about squash, the upcoming school year, and what my schedule was going to look like. After what felt like a quick nap (my parents say I slept for hours), I woke up to my father pulling the car into my dorm room parking lot. I walked right upstairs to my room, Dana 222, and only then did I truly realize that my life was going to change. I could not believe that I was going to live the next year of my life in such a cramped and small space. My roommate and I arranged our beds and tidied up the rest of our room. I took a deep breath and looked at my parents. Twenty years had gone by in the blink of an eye. Boy was I going to miss them...

Before I knew it, it was time to say goodbye. I walked my parents to the back of my dorm building and hugged them. I started to cry as I told them I loved them. I wished them a safe trip home as they got in the car and sped off. I looked at their car, in the process of leaving the lot, and took a second to reflect on what my life had evolved into. Colby was the start of a new chapter for me. I was all alone in a new place with new people. None of them even knew about my stroke. I wondered how the conversation would go. *Would I tell people my secret? Would it ever even come up?* I went back to my room and organized all of my school necessities. I did not know if I was ready for this new chapter of my life, but I had to give it a shot.

Fortunately, I met some new friends in my first week on campus and became close with my teammates almost immediately. It was nice to go into college as part of a team because it meant that I had a friend group from the start. And though I liked my new friends, I was not happy for the two first two months at school. I missed my family, I missed my brother, and I missed my sister. I missed Rocky, and I missed my home. At the time, I was not enjoying school at all.

Despite only taking four courses, I found myself swimming in a mountain of work pretty quickly. I was naive to think that Colby would not be academically rigorous. When I found myself spending almost every night in the library, I decided to enlist the help of one of Colby's learning specialists. The specialist, Antoine Morin, and I immediately clicked. In our weekly meetings, we went over everything from my daily schedule to my individual assignments. Without him, I would have been lost. I genuinely believe he was the sole reason why I was able to balance a demanding workload with my athletic schedule. We went through my classes one by one and always made a checklist for the work I had yet to accomplish. All in all, he has helped me an unbelievable amount. I am and will always be thankful.

At the end of the summer, Coach Khan retired from his position as the head squash coach at Colby College. The news came as a shock to my new teammates and me. We were definitely sad to see him go. As a result, the men's and women's squash teams partnered with the athletic department to interview potential candidates from the start of the school year well into October. We eventually decided on Chris Abplanalp, the former head coach from Saint Lawrence University. He is a great guy, a great coach, and an incredibly successful recruiter. He joined Colby and looked to make an impact in college squash with our team right from the start.

By the end of the fall, I came to realize that I was now a full-blown college student. And although I grew comfortable with my schedule, I struggled to find ways to conceal my stroke. I was constantly afraid that my friends would find out about it and prayed they would not judge me. I did not want them to think that I was different, or that I was weird. The problems started when I wore flip-flops around campus. The questions came out of nowhere. My friends asked why my ankle looked swollen, why I looked like I was limping, and why my right calf was so much smaller than my left one. It was difficult to deal with, but I slowly realized that the questions were just the beginning. The scariest part of keeping my stroke a secret was showering in the locker room with my teammates. I always had to be the first one in the showers and the last one out or the last one in the showers and the last one out. There was no in-between. If I was not, I would get bombarded with questions from around the locker room. "Hey man, are you okay? What's up with the ankle? Go see a trainer, man, are you serious?" The questions never stopped, but I did not care. I knew that I would tell my teammates when it was the right time for me. I was not ready. I had yet to accomplish my goal.

At Coach Abplanlp's first day at practice, he immediately commented on my right ankle and the disproportionate size of my calves. I tried to be forthright and answer his questions on the spot, but eventually ended up having to tell him about my disability in a private meeting later that week. I told him that I suffered a stroke during birth and that I may never get better. Surprisingly, he was unbelievably supportive. He started to set up meetings for me with our new strength and conditioning coach, Matt, and told me that he would not treat me any different from the rest of the players on the team. I would have to compete for my spot, just like everyone else. I was thankful; he gave me the chance that I needed. I was so close to accomplishing my dream. I was so close to fulfilling a promise that I made to myself years earlier when I was lonelier and more depressed than ever. He helped me make my dream come true.

My teammates and I spent the last couple weeks of the fall preparing for our upcoming season. It proved to be a turning point in Colby squash's history not only because we hired a new coach, but also because we had five freshmen on the men's team who were projected to play in the top ten. In those workouts, I found out that college tryouts were going to be much different than my high school's had been. Everyone had to compete for their spot. Coach Abplanalp held a meeting before the start of tryouts and told our team that each player would just end up playing every teammates with a similar skill level. Our team was too small to do a round-robin. I could not wait to get on court and compete. In the tryouts, I won two of my opening three matches and found myself in a good position to make the top 9. The competition was fierce, but I played each match with a crazy focus and desire. I ended the tryouts by grinding out a hard-fought win against a fellow freshman. I was so close to my dream; I had to make sure that it was going to come true. I won the match 11 - 8 in the fifth game and secured the #7 position on the ladder. And even though I was not outwardly enthusiastic at the time, I have never wanted anything more in my life. I could not wait to play my first collegiate match.

The morning of November 11, 2018, was one of the happiest and most memorable moments of my life. It was the date of our first match. We were scheduled to play away at Tufts University, but ended up

The First Twenty

playing the match at Harvard's Murr Center because Tufts does not have home courts. My teammates and I arrived at Harvard by bus at about 8:30 AM for a 10 AM match. We disembarked, immediately got on court, and started to stretch and warm up. I was very apprehensive. Since the women's team always plays before the men's, I sat on the bleachers and rolled out my ankle before the match. Although there were not many spectators in the stands, the venue was incredible. I could not have pictured a better way for my dream to come true. As the women's matches ended, I sat in the locker room and listened to my favorite artist, Jack Johnson, on repeat to calm me down. It was almost time...

Unfortunately, neither of my parents were able to attend the match because I, stupidly, gave them an incorrect start time. It was upsetting; I still regret not being able to share such a critical moment in my life with them. Nevertheless, I finished my warmup and strolled on court for introductions. I can still recall the first time my captain, Elliot Gross, called my name in lineups. "Now playing number seven for the Colby Mules... Tyler Burt!" I shook my opponent's hand, the opposing coach's hand, and then joined my team in the huddle. My opponent, Will Dewire, was a product of the Gilman school and we had split two matches when we played each other in high school competition. But I did not care about the past or about who was projected to win; I was ready. I could not wait to get on court.

Going into the match, I thought that it was going to be a dogfight, but I was wrong. Will won the racket spin and proceeded to serve. He served the ball to my backhand, and I was forced to counter with a crosscourt that sent him deep into the back left corner. He quickly cut off my crosscourt and went short with a straight volley drop. I do not think he was expecting me to get to the ball because of my mobility issues, but I proved him wrong. I got to his shot in the front left corner and decided to go back to my "bread and butter" to win the point. I positioned my body so that he could not see the ball from the "T" and played a frontcourt trickle boast. I recovered back to the middle of the court in the nick of time and looked up. He did not even attempt to make a move; he kind just stood there. I had just won the first point of the match.

Tears started to well up in the corner of my eyes. I did it; I had just accomplished my goal. It was possible that I had just become the first-ever stroke survivor to compete in men's Division I athletics. I could not have been more proud of myself. I started to raise my hands in jubilation but thought better of it at the last second. I did not want my opponent to think that I was mocking him; I mean it was only the first point of the match. Nobody even clapped when the first point ended. I did not blame them; they knew nothing about the obstacles that I had overcome to put myself in the position that I was in.

Sadly, my internal celebration did not last long. Will was upset about losing the first point and came back with a vengeance. He decided to stop going short for the rest of the game and started hitting every other ball to my deep backhand. He took a lead and never looked back. I tried my best to keep up with him and continue fighting but had little success. He ended up taking the first game 11 - 7 and the match 3 - 0. I was shocked; I felt like the match was over before I could even take a second to breathe. It was exhausting. The moment I shook Will's hand, I started to tear up. I was overcome with emotion. I could not believe what I had just accomplished. I exited the court and tried to sprint to the locker room without being noticed by any of my teammates. I grabbed my phone on the way out and frantically called my parents. As I got to the locker room, I sat in the corner and threw my shirt over my head. I broke down as I told my parents about the match. I had just officially become a college athlete. Of course, my parents loved and congratulated me, but I do not think they understood the magnitude of my accomplishment at the time. In many ways, I am exactly like my father. I love sports, I love to compete, and I wanted to prove to myself, my father, and everyone else, that I could be successful in sports despite my disability. I could barely choke the words out. I had just proven to myself that I was stronger than anything a bully could ever do to me. I proved all of my skeptics wrong; I was not a failure. I accomplished the impossible. I pulled myself together. I knew that I had nothing left to prove, I mean I had already achieved my dream, but I realized that I did not want my college career to end with a loss. I was part of a team, and I wanted to stay a part of a team. I told myself that I was going to play out the entire season. I wanted to prove to everyone that most limitations are self-imposed. I was not going to let my stroke define me.

The following weekend, my teammates and I played matches against Hobart, Dickinson, and Connecticut College at Wesleyan

The First Twenty

University as part of their round-robin tournament. We arrived at the courts late on a Friday night and played our first match against Hobart. My teammates and I were rusty because we had just gotten off the bus, but we managed to pull out a victory. I played in the #7 position against Christian Escalona, a junior from Hobart. I won the match 3 – 0 and secured my first ever college victory. Even though I celebrated with my teammates after the match, there was still more work to be done. We advanced to the next round and played our second round of matches against the higher-ranked Dickinson Red Devils. I played an old friend, Henry Smith, and unfortunately lost the match 11 - 9 in the fifth game. It was a tough loss, but I was able to bounce back. Our team finished the weekend with a 9 - 0 victory over Connecticut College. We dominated from start to finish. I won my match 3 - 0. Everyone was in good spirits because of the win, and we joked with each other for the entire bus ride home. And even though I was excited to come out of the weekend with a winning record, I could not wait to compete against higher-ranked teams.

My teammates and I traveled to Middlebury and Williams on January 13 to play our second weekend of matches. Both Middlebury and Williams were ranked much higher than our team in the country, but I welcomed the challenge. I did not know what I was getting myself into. My opponents, Nate Moll and Ben Eisenberg, started the match on fire, made quick work of me, and did not let up. They beat me 3 - 0, 3 - 0. I was upset, and yet there was really nothing that I could do. My opponents were much more experienced and much more skilled than me. I felt more vulnerable than ever. Nate exposed my disability and moved me around the court with ease. I was not able to keep up. I came off of the court gasping for air. It was not the way that I pictured my weekend going.

Two days later, I tried to bounce back in our first and only home match of the year against Bates College, but I was unsuccessful. My opponent, McLeod Abbott, took an offensive position on the "T" right from the start and forced me to commit unforced error after unforced error. In retrospect, he did not do anything special to win. He simply hit drive after drive, and waited for me to commit the unforced error. Stupidly, I fell right into his trap. I lost the match 3 - 1 and could not wait to get off court. I was embarrassed. I should have performed better. All of my new friends came to the match and would not stop talking about my ankle. "What's good with your ankle?" "Why don't you get that fixed?" "Go to the trainer... now. Man, c'mon!" I tried to dodge the questions as best I could and scampered back to the locker room.

Our next tournament was a round-robin at Drexel University in Philadelphia. And even though I loved seeing my family, the bus ride down was long and cramped. That weekend, we were scheduled to play matches against Franklin and Marshall, the University of Virginia, Drexel, and the University of Pennsylvania. I was excited to get on court, I had a feeling that these matches would be similar to the ones our team had played against Middlebury and Williams. We came into every match as the underdog, and honestly, it was for a good reason. My teammates and I lost all of ours matches that weekend. I lost 3 - 0 to Franklin and Marshall, 3 - 0 to Drexel, 3 - 0 to the University of Pennsylvania, and 3 - 1 to the University of Virginia. It was not the way that I wanted the weekend to go, but I tried to take it as a learning experience and move on. The NESCAC tournament was up next.

On February 1, my teammates and I played our first round of the NESCAC tournament against Connecticut College. They were seeded 8th, and my teammates and I looked to replicate our performance against them from the Wesleyan round-robin. Thankfully, I was able to forget about my losses from the previous weekend and played reasonably well. I won my match 11 - 2 in the fifth game, and our team won 9 - 0. We were excited, but our enthusiasm did not last for long. We had to play Trinity in the next round. The Trinity team was the defending national champions, and their players quickly dismantled my teammates and me. We lost 9 - 0 in a blowout. I do not think any of my teammates even got a game; they were just that good. With the win, Trinity knocked us out of the NESCAC tournament. We bused back to Colby the next day and prepared for our last tournament of the year, the collegiate national championships.

On February 15, my teammates and I played in the collegiate National Championships at Yale University. Upon entering the venue, I found the atmosphere exhilarating. It immediately brought back memories of not only high school, but middle school as well. I had a fantastic time reconnecting with old friends and seeing my parents. They made the trip up from Philadelphia to watch me play in my final tournament of the year; it was so great to see them. My teammates and

The First Twenty

I started the tournament with a 9 - 0 win against Bucknell University and continued with a 9 - 0 win against Hobart. And though both of my matches were relatively easy, I took the first match 3 - 1 and the second match 3 - 0. I was excited when we beat Hobart because I had begun to realize how much my hard work had paid off. I was winning most of my matches toward the end of the season.

In the third round, we were scheduled to play our final match of the tournament against Dickinson. My teammates and I went into the match looking to avenge our loss from the Wesleyan round-robin, but unfortunately, the match did not go as planned. Even though my team fought hard, I found myself stepping on court with the match already decided. We were down 8 - 0; we had already lost. It was unbelievably disappointing. And although there was no pressure on me to win, I choked the match. I lost 11 - 6 in the fourth game. I was pissed. My teammates and I went into our final match looking to get revenge against Dickinson from earlier in the year, and yet we lost by more the second time than we did the first time. It was tough to swallow. Needless to say, it was not the way that I wanted to end such an important season.

As the winter winded down, my team and I began spending more time together off of the court. We still played matches against each other and worked out together, but it was not the same grind that we had to endure while in season. I found myself spending more time in the library and was fortunate to meet new friends outside of the squash team. I continued my weekly sessions with Antoine and created a plan for each of my second-semester classes. I am so happy to have him in my corner for the next three years—he is remarkable at his job. As I reflect on my first year at Colby, I am appreciative of my teammates, my friends, my teachers, my coach, and the tutors that I had throughout the year. I am proud to say that my teammates have become some of my best friends. My freshman year at Colby was the birth of a new beginning. It was a year of personal triumph, my first year of living on my own, and my first step towards life as an adult. I could not be more excited for what the future holds.

Moving Forward

I wanted to write this book for two reasons.

First, I would like to thank everyone who helped me achieve my lifelong dream of becoming a Division 1 athlete. To my parents, what can I say? I would not be in the position that I am in without your love and support. You both mean the world to me. To my brother and sister, thank you for always having my back and supporting me. I love you both. To my extended family, thank you for accepting me despite my disability. Your support has helped me break out of my shell and become my own man. To my teammates and coach Abplanalp, thank you for treating me as if I was one of your own and accepting me from the moment I arrived on Colby's campus. To the Haverford School, thank you for instilling an unrelenting work ethic in me and for teaching me never to give up. To the Scozzie Squash Academy and Paul Frank, thank you for never giving up on me and for treating me like family. I will always be grateful. To my doctors: Whoeling and Nichols, thank you for being with me every step of the way. I would not be here today without both of you. To Chris Lengthorn, thank you for always being a resource to me. You elevated my squash game to new heights. I am, and will always be, grateful. To Darrin and Maximum Performance International, thank you for always getting my body right, and for taking me in right from the start. I appreciate you all more than you could ever know. And lastly, to my childhood friends, words cannot begin to explain how much you guys have done for me. I love you guys.

I also wanted to write this book to show every kid out there that you can accomplish more than you ever thought possible. All you need is a work ethic and a great attitude. Never, ever give up; I believe in you. I mean, if I can do it, I promise you that you can too.

T.

Made in the USA
Middletown, DE
01 September 2019